SOCIAL CONVENTIONS

•¶MP•

PRINCETON MONOGRAPHS
IN PHILOSOPHY

Harry Frankfurt, Series Editor

———————————— ◦ ҶMP ◦ ————————————

The Princeton Monographs in Philosophy series offers short
historical and systematic studies on a wide variety
of philosophical topics.

SOCIAL
CONVENTIONS

FROM LANGUAGE TO LAW

Andrei Marmor

PRINCETON UNIVERSITY PRESS

PRINCETON AND OXFORD

Published by Princeton University Press, 41 William Street,
Princeton, New Jersey 08540
In the United Kingdom: Princeton University Press, 6 Oxford
Street, Woodstock, Oxfordshire OX20 1TW

Library of Congress Cataloging-in-Publication Data

Marmor, Andrei.
Social conventions : from language to law / Andrei Marmor.
p. cm. — (Princeton monographs in philosophy)
Includes bibliographical references (p. 177) and index.
ISBN 978-0-691-14090-2 (cl.: alk. paper)
1. Convention (Philosophy) 2. Social sciences—Philosophy.
3. Language and languages—Philosophy. I. Title.
B809.15.M37 2009
323.01'4—dc22
2008055165

British Library Cataloging-in-Publication Data is available

This book has been composed in Janson Text

Printed on acid-free paper. ∞

press.princeton.edu

Printed in the United States of America

1 3 5 7 9 10 8 6 4 2

Contents

Acknowledgments vii

Preface ix

CHAPTER ONE
A First Look at the Nature of Conventions 1

CHAPTER TWO
Constitutive Conventions 31

CHAPTER THREE
Deep Conventions 58

CHAPTER FOUR
Conventions of Language: Semantics 79

CHAPTER FIVE
Conventions of Language: Pragmatics 106

CHAPTER SIX
The Morality of Conventions 131

CHAPTER SEVEN
The Conventional Foundations of Law 155

Bibliography 177

Index 183

Acknowledgments

SOME of my previous publications on conventions are incorporated in this work, all in substantially revised form. Chapter 1 draws on material published in two articles: "On Convention," *Synthese* 107 (1996): 349, and "Deep Conventions," *Philosophy and Phenomenological Research* 74 (2007): 586. Chapter 3 also draws on the latter article. Chapter 2 incorporates some ideas I have published in my *Positive Law and Objective Values* (Oxford, 2001). Chapter 4, which was originally written for this book, appeared in a modified, article version, in a special issue of *Topoi*: "Convention: An Interdisciplinary Study," 27 (2008): 101. Finally, chapter 7 incorporates, with substantial revisions, some of the material I have published in "How Law Is Like Chess," *Legal Theory* 12 (2006): 347.

Preface

SOCIAL conventions pervade almost every aspect of our lives. Everywhere you look, you see conventions we follow. Of course, in reading these words you already employ numerous conventions of the English language. But let me walk you through an ordinary day, just to see how ubiquitous conventions are. Perhaps your day begins by (conventionally) greeting your spouse and kids as you wake them up for breakfast. After breakfast, you dress for work, more or less complying with current conventions of fashion. Then you drive to work, on your way following rules and conventions of the road. Outside your office, you meet one of your colleagues and pause to exchange some polite (conventional) niceties. In your office, the phone rings, you pick it up and say "Hello," since this is the relevant convention.

At some point you begin grading the papers that have been piling up on your desk, bearing in mind that there are conventions about grades you need to comply with. To cheer yourself up, perhaps you think about the theater performance you saw last night, or the golf you plan on playing next Saturday—both activities conventionally regulated, of course. When the grading is finished, you tell yourself, you will begin work on this new article you have been hoping to write. Luckily, you don't have to figure out from scratch how to construct an academic article. After all, there are some conventions about this.

As you can see, there is hardly any activity that is not at least partly regulated by social conventions. In some cases it is clear that the practice is conventional. In other cases, the convention-ality is controversial. Consider natural language, for example. Certain aspects of language are conventional, such as sound-sense relations, spelling of words, surface rules of grammar, and so on. But what about deeper aspects of language, are they conventional as well? Are aspects of morality conventionally de-termined? Is arithmetic conventional? On these questions con-troversies rage. The fact that conventionality is controversial suggests that we need a clear view of what conventional rules are, what makes them unique, and what makes it philosophi-cally sensible to have the kind of controversies we do about the conventionality of this or that aspect of our social lives.

This book provides a detailed account of the nature of con-ventions. In the first part of the book, which spans the first three chapters, I propose a general account of what conven-tions are. The second part of the book, chapters 4–7, applies this account to the domains of language, morality, and law.

This is a short book, and there is no need to give it a long introduction. There are, however, two related points I need to clarify in advance. First, I take it that conventions are a species of norms; they are rules that regulate human conduct. As such, conventions pose a problem that is best cast in terms of practi-cal reasoning. If there is anything unique about conventional norms, there must be something unique about the ways in which they figure in our practical reasons. The second assump-tion is precisely the idea that conventional norms are unique. In spite of the great diversity of domains in which we follow conventions, they share an essential feature, namely, their arbi-trariness. To suggest that a certain norm is conventional is to suggest that in some sense it just happens to be the one we fol-low, that we could have followed a different norm instead, that is, without any significant loss of purpose. This arbitrary feature of conventional norms is both a challenge and the beginning of an explanation. It is a challenge to explain the practical reasons for following a rule that is, basically, arbitrary. But the arbitrary nature of conventions is also the beginning of an explanation of why it matters, philosophically speaking, to determine whether a certain domain, or type of norms, is conventional or not. It matters precisely because conventionality entails a certain arbitrariness, suggesting that the way things are could have been different in a real sense. Colloquially, this intuition is often expressed by saying that this or that is "merely conventional." A good philosophical insight is suggested by this colloquialism: a practical domain that is conventionally determined is one that could have been different from the way it is, without any significant loss in its point, purpose, or value. More precisely, as I will suggest throughout this work, the conventionality of a domain is closely tied with crucial elements of contingency, path dependency, and underdetermination by reasons. These are the features that make it philosophically interesting to determine whether a certain set of norms is conventional or not. The purpose of the first part of the book is to explain and defend these general points. The purpose of the second part is to demonstrate that we can apply such a theory of conventionality to a wide range of domains, thereby getting a better sense of their relative contingency and the extent to which those domains are determined by reasons.

To give a very brief description of the chapters: the first one provides a detailed definition of social conventions, explaining David Lewis's rationale of conventional rules and the limits of his account. Chapter 2 considerably extends Lewis's account, arguing that in addition to the coordination conventions he has identified, there is another important type of conventions whose main function is to constitute social practices. Chapter 3 presents the idea that there is a distinction between deep and surface conventions, and explains what deep conventions are. Subsequently, chapters 4 and 5 are about the conventional aspects of language: Chapter 4 considers the question of whether the literal meaning of words in a natural language is conventional or not, arguing that somewhat less is conventional about meaning than is usually assumed. Chapter 5 takes up some of the pragmatic aspects of language use, considering the possible roles of conventions in two main areas: implicatures and speech acts. (Those whose main interest in conventions derives from their interest in language can stop reading at this point. Those who are not particularly interested in language can skip chapters

4 and 5.) Chapter 6 focuses on the relations between conventions and morality: first, it examines the kind of moral reasons we may have for following social conventions, drawing on some of the distinctions introduced in chapter 2; second, it examines the various roles that conventions, including deep conventions, play in the moral domain, arguing that these roles are important but also somewhat limited. Chapter 7 argues for a certain conception of the conventional foundations of law, based on some of the distinctions presented in chapters 2 and 3.

My concern with understanding conventions begins with an interest in practical reasons. That is where I think we should start, and it is where this book ends. Somewhere along the way, however, we face the challenge of understanding the role of conventions in shaping natural language. I believe that we have two main reasons to be interested in the conventionality of language: First, because language is a central case, and thus important as a test for any theory of conventions. A theory of conventions that cannot be employed to show which aspects of language are conventional, and why, fails in its claim to generality. Second, there is an inherent interest, I believe, in trying to unravel those aspects of language that are conventional from those that are not; given the arbitrary nature of conventions, our ability to identify the conventional aspects of language should tell us something of interest about the nature of language itself.

In the course of writing this book I was extremely fortunate to be helped by friends and colleagues. A particular debt of gratitude I owe to Scott Soames; without his endless patience and detailed comments on my drafts, I could not have completed this project. Many others commented on parts of this work over the years, and I am very grateful to them all. They include Tim Williamson, Joseph Raz, Leslie Green, Jeff King, Mark Schroeder, Gideon Yaffe, Martin Stone, David Enoch, Alon Harel, and Scott Altman. For their invaluable comments and suggestions I am also very grateful to the anonymous referees who reviewed the manuscript for Princeton University Press.

SOCIAL CONVENTIONS

————————•ꟼMꟼ•————————

CHAPTER ONE

A First Look at the Nature of Conventions

I WANT to begin with an attempt to define what social conventions are. I will start with some intuitive ideas on what seems special about conventional norms, and try to define those features as precisely as possible. If this tack leads us to a single explanation of the point, or function, of conventions in our lives, so be it. But we should not assume in advance that a single explanation is available, and we should certainly not predetermine what it is.

First, conventional rules are, in a specific sense, *arbitrary*. Roughly, if a rule is a convention, we should be able to point to an alternative rule we could have followed to achieve basically the same purpose. Second, conventional rules normally lose their point if they are not *actually followed* in the relevant community. The reasons for following a rule that is conventional are tied to the fact that others (in the relevant population) follow it too. To give one familiar example, consider the convention of saying "Hello" when responding to a telephone call. Both features are manifest in this example. The purpose of the convention is to have a recognizable expression that indicates to the caller that someone has answered the phone. But of course, using the particular expression "Hello" is arbitrary; any other similar expression would serve just as well—that is, as long as the expression I use is one that others use too. If the point of the convention is to have an expression that can be quickly recognized, then people have a reason to follow the norm, that is, use the expression, that others in the community follow as well. If, for some reason, people no longer use this expression, I no longer have a reason to use it either.

In fact, both of these intuitive features of conventional rules derive from a single, though complex, feature that I will call "conventionality," defined as follows:

> A rule, R, is conventional, if and only if all the following conditions obtain:
>
> 1. There is a group of people, a population, P, that normally follow R in circumstances C.
> 2. There is a reason, or a combination of reasons, call it A, for members of P to follow R in circumstances C.
> 3. There is at least one other potential rule, S, that if members of P had actually followed in circumstances C, then A would have been a sufficient reason for members of P to follow S instead of R in circumstances C, and at least partly because S is the rule generally followed instead of R. The rules R and S are such that it is impossible (or pointless) to comply with both of them concomitantly in circumstances C.

In this chapter I will explain and defend this definition, showing how it applies to the variety of conventions we are familiar with. I will then present David Lewis's theory of social conventions, arguing that it successfully explains some cases, but that it fails in many others. Finally, I will consider Margaret Gilbert's alternative account of conventions, arguing that it raises more questions than it answers. An alternative to Lewis's theory or, more precisely, a supplement to it, will be presented in the next chapter.

DEFINITION

Let us take up the details of the definition.

> 1. There is a group of people, a population, P, that normally follow R in circumstances C.

This condition indicates that conventions are *social rules*:[1] A convention is a rule that is, by and large, followed by a population. Not all rules have to meet this condition. People can formulate rules of action and regard them as binding even if nobody is actually following those rules. Conventions, however, must be practiced, that is, actually followed, by a population in order to exist. Furthermore, I use the term "followed" advisedly. In many contexts people's behavior can conform to a rule without the rule being followed, as such. A rule is followed when it is regarded as binding. Conventions, I assume, must be regarded as binding by the relevant population. To say that a certain behavior is conventional is to assume that, at least upon reflection, people would say that they behave in a certain way because the relevant conduct is required by the convention.

Margaret Gilbert raised some doubts about this, relying on the following counterexample: suppose that it has been a convention in a certain community that people should send thank-you notes after being invited to dinner parties. As it happens, conformity with this convention has dwindled and most people no longer abide by it. Either they tend to express their gratitude in some other way, or not at all. "Does *this* mean that there is no longer a convention [to send thank-you notes]?" Gilbert asks. "The present author has no such clear sense," she replies.[2]

---

[1] A note on usage: I assume here that "rule" is the content of a linguistic form and thus that rules can be valid or correct irrespective of practice. Paradigmatic example of rules would be rules of conduct, such as "In circumstances C do X." Later we will have to include more complex rules, including those that determine how to create or modify other rules. The word "norm" I will use to indicate a rule that is followed by a population or, at least, is regarded as binding by a population. Thus the terms "social rule" and "norm" will be used interchangeably.

[2] See Gilbert, *On Social Facts*, 347. Notably, at other places in the same chapter (e.g., 345), Gilbert is more explicit in claiming that conventions can exist without conformity of behavior. See also Millikan, "Language Conventions Made Simple," 170, who seems to share that view. Millikan's examples, however, are somewhat ambiguous. ("Few actually hand out cigars at the birth of a boy, nor does everyone wear green on St. Patrick's Day, or decorate with red and green on Christmas" [170].) Either they are like Gilbert's, namely, conventions that have, by and large, ceased to be practiced, or else, they concern

The lack of a clear sense about such cases is understandable. It often happens that a conventional rule gradually ceases to be practiced, and at some point it might become impossible to determine whether the convention still exists or not. In other words, the idea of a practice is rather vague, and borderline cases are not uncommon. As with most distinctions, however, the vagueness of the concepts constituting the distinction does not entail that the distinction itself is problematic. The importance of this first condition pertains to the unique structure of reasons for following rules that are conventional. It is a unique feature of such reasons that they are closely tied to the fact that others generally comply with the rule. This will become clearer as we complete the explanation. Suffice it to say at this point that Gilbert's example is not a counterexample to condition 1; what we face here is precisely what is described, namely, a convention that has dwindled. There used to be such a conventional practice, but now it is no longer clear that there is one. The essential point remains that conventional rules are social rules and that there must be a community that by and large follows the rule for it to be conventional.

Similar considerations apply to the question of what constitutes a community that practices a certain convention. Some conventions are practiced almost universally; others are much more parochial. However, a rule followed by just a few people is typically not a convention, even if the other conditions obtain. As social rules, conventions must be practiced by some significant number of people. Numbers matter here because in small numbers the relevant agents can create, modify, or abolish the rules at will, by simple agreements between them. As David Lewis was right to observe, conventions typically emerge as an alternative to agreements, precisely in those cases where agreements are difficult to obtain because of the large number of agents involved.

cases in which only a small part of the general population actually conforms to the convention. Naturally, it all depends on how one identifies the relevant population. Either the convention, e.g., to hand out cigars at the birth of a boy, is one that has dwindled and no longer practiced, and therefore, is no longer a convention, or else it is a convention that is practiced by a small subset of the general population, as the case may be.

(More on this below.) But again, the concept of a population or a community is vague, and borderline cases are bound to exist.

2. There is a reason, or a combination of reasons, call it A, for members of P to follow R in circumstances C.

The second condition requires three clarifications. First, what is a *reason* for following a rule? I take it that reasons for action are facts that count in favor (or against) doing (or not doing) something. Thus reasons for action are closely tied with the idea of value. A reason to φ typically derives from the fact that φ-ing is good, valuable, or serves some worthy end. Some philosophers claim that it is the other way around: to say of something that it is valuable is to say that it has certain properties that provide reasons for action.[3] Either way, reasons are closely related to values or goodness. A reason to follow a rule necessarily assumes (or, is suggested by the assumption) that following the rule is valuable under the circumstances, that it serves some purpose or point, that it is good in some respect (not necessarily moral, of course).[4]

Second, it is not part of this condition of conventionality that members of P must be aware of the reason, A, to follow R. People may follow conventional rules for various misconceived reasons or, in fact, for no reason that is apparent to them at all. The conventionality of a rule does not depend on the subjective conception of the reasons for following the rule by those who follow it. As an example, consider this: there are some Orthodox Jewish communities who believe that Hebrew is a holy language descended directly from God. In fact, they only speak Hebrew in religious contexts, and use Yiddish for

---

[3] Roughly, this is Scanlon's view, called the "buck passing" account of values. See Scanlon, *What We Owe to Each Other*, 96–97. The details of Scanlon's view are controversial; see, for example, Heuer, "Explaining Reasons."

[4] This formulation assumes that there is a fact of the matter about reasons for action, as about some matters of value. (For an argument that the latter does not necessarily assume *realism* about values, seem my *Positive Law and Objective Values*, chap. 6.) This objectivist assumption is not necessary for the rest of the argument in this book. Expressivists can follow the argument on their own terms.

everyday life. Surely Hebrew remains conventional (to the extent that it is, of course), even when spoken by those Orthodox Jews. The fact that they misconceive the reasons for following the rules does not prove the contrary. Reasons for following a convention do not have to be transparent.

Similar considerations apply to the question of whether people have to know that the rule they follow is a convention or not. Lewis suggested that at least in one crucial sense, the answer is yes.[5] He claimed that, for the rule to be conventional, the arbitrary nature of the rule must be *common knowledge* in the relevant population. Tyler Burge has rightly argued that this is wrong and no such condition should form part of the definition. People can be simply mistaken about the conventional nature of the rules they follow. To mention one of Burge's examples, he asks us to imagine a small, completely isolated linguistic community, none of whose members ever heard anyone speaking a different language. "Such a community would not know—or perhaps even have reason to believe—that there are humanly possible alternatives to speaking their language. . . . Yet we have no inclination to deny that their language is conventional. They are simply wrong about the nature of their activities."[6] Notably, such mistakes can go both ways; for example, some people believe that all moral norms are social conventions. They may be quite wrong.

There is, really, nothing surprising about the fact that conventionality is often opaque. The conventionality of various domains, or types of norms, could not be controversial had it been the case that conventionality is necessarily transparent. However, the fact that people need not be aware of the correct reasons for following a convention, or even of the fact that it is a conventional rule they follow, does not entail that there are no epistemic constraints that apply to conventionality of norms. The idea of following a rule, in itself, is a rather complex condition. It normally entails that the agent regards the rule as binding under the circumstances, which would normally entail that the agent must be aware of the

---

5 Lewis, *Convention*, 58.
6 Burge, "On Knowledge and Convention," 250.

fact that he or she is following a rule. It may be tempting to think that people can act in ways which conform to a convention without it being the case that in this they follow a rule. According to this line of thought, then, conformity to a convention is not always a matter of following a rule. There is, I think, some truth in this, but only in a very limited sense. We often follow norms without being self-consciously aware of the fact that we do so. In reading these words you follow numerous norms of the English language (notation of symbols, spelling, meaning, syntax, etc.). It is not something you do in a self-conscious way; you don't tell yourself that the symbol "A" stands for a particular sound, that "B" stands for a different sound, and so on. Following a rule does not require that the agent be self-consciously aware of the fact that he or she follows the rule. But in using these symbols in reading or writing, we do follow rules, and, generally speaking, we know that we do. We normally become aware of the fact that we follow a rule when our attention is drawn to it by some particular need, say, when there is a question about what the rule is, or how to interpret it under some doubtful circumstances. None of this proves, of course, that conventions are necessarily rules. I will deal with this question shortly. The point here is that to the extent that conventions are rules, and to the extent that conformity to a convention is an instance of following a norm, there is always the *potential* of awareness that in complying with a convention one follows a rule. But again, what the reasons for the rule are, or what kind of rule it is, is not something that the agents must be aware of.

The assumption that there must be a reason for following a rule that is a convention requires another clarification. On the one hand, it is normally the case that people follow rules for reasons. On the other hand, we must make room for the possibility that a convention is silly or just plain wrong. There would seem to be two ways to account for this. In many cases it would be appropriate to say that there is a reason to follow a convention, R, but there are also reasons not to follow R, and perhaps the latter ought to prevail. A reason to follow a rule does not entail an all-things-considered judgment that one ought to follow it. Second, it might be the case that the reason to follow the convention is just not a good reason. But this is problematic: according to a plausible view about the nature of reasons, there is no such thing as a bad reason (just as there is no such thing as a bad value). Either there is a reason, or there isn't. If this is correct (and I think that it is), then we cannot say that there is a reason to follow a convention that is just a bad reason; we would have to say that there is a reason, perhaps a very weak one, that is somehow immediately defeated by countervailing considerations.

The third condition explains the sense in which conventional rules are *arbitrary* and, as we shall see, *compliance dependent*:

> 3. There is at least one other potential rule, S, that if members of P had actually followed in circumstances C, then A would have been a sufficient reason for members of P to follow S instead of R in circumstances C, and at least partly because S is the rule generally followed instead of R. The rules R and S are such that it is impossible (or pointless) to comply with both of them concomitantly in circumstances C.

As David Lewis explained in his account of social conventions, it is crucial to note that arbitrariness (thus defined) should not be confused with indifference.[7] This condition does not entail that people who follow the convention ought to be indifferent about the choice between R and S. The rule is arbitrary, in the requisite sense, even if people do have a reason to prefer one over the other, but only as long as the reason to prefer one of the potential rules is not stronger than the reason to follow the rule that is actually followed by others. A typical game theory model of this is the so-called battle of the sexes game (which Lewis calls an imperfect coordination problem). Assume two agents, X and Y, both having a dominant preference to act in concert with the other; however, X prefers option P over Q, and Y prefers option Q over P. As long as their dominant preference is to act in concert with each other (namely, if Y opts for Q, X would rather Q as well, even though he would have preferred P; and same goes for Y), the condition of arbitrariness

---

7 See Lewis, *Convention*, 76–80.

as defined above is satisfied. Consider, for example, the case of a greeting convention. Suppose that there is a reason to greet acquaintances in some conventional manner. Now let us assume, for the sake of simplicity, that there are only two possible alternatives: we can either greet each other by shaking hands, or else by just nodding our head. Presumably, some people would prefer the hand-shaking option, while others (perhaps because they are not so keen on physical contact) would prefer nodding. The point is that we need not assume indifference. As long as the reason to act in concert with others is stronger than people's preference for one of the options, whichever rule evolves as the common practice is likely to be followed. And it would be arbitrary in the sense defined here.[8]

In a sense, then, arbitrariness admits of degrees. We could say that a rule is completely arbitrary if the reason to follow it entails complete indifference between the rule, R, that people do follow, and its alternative(s), S, that they could have followed instead, achieving the same purpose. Then a rule becomes less and less arbitrary as we move away from complete indifference, up to the point at which the reason to follow the rule that is actually followed by others is just slightly stronger than the reason to prefer a different alternative.

Arbitrariness is an essential, defining feature, of conventional rules.[9] This is actually a twofold condition. First, a rule is arbitrary if it has a conceivable alternative. If a rule does not have an alternative that could have been followed instead without a significant loss in its function or purpose, then it is not a convention. Norms of rationality, and basic moral norms, for instance, are not conventions; properly defined and qualified, they do not

---

[8] As we shall see later, the rationale of following arbitrary rules is not confined to coordination situations. For a much more sophisticated game-theoretical treatment of these issues, see, for example, Sugden, *Economics of Rights*, and Vanderschraaf, "Convention as Correlated Equilibrium."

[9] This is undoubtedly one of the most important insights of Lewis's account, an insight that is shared by most of his critics. (See, for example, Millikan, "Conventions of Language Made Simple.") A notable exception is Miller, "Conventions, Interdependence of Action, and Collective Ends." Gilbert also disagrees, and I will consider her alternative account at the end of this chapter.

admit of alternatives (in the sense defined above).[10] Admittedly, it is not easy to define what a relevant alternative to a rule might be. Surely not every imaginable alternative to a rule would satisfy this condition. First, it has to be a rule that the same population could have followed in the same circumstances. Second, it has to be an alternative rule that is supported by the same reasons or functions that the original rule serves for the relevant population. Third, in some loose sense that I cannot define here, the alternative rule has to be one that the relevant population can actually follow so that the cost of following it would not exceed the rule's benefits. Finally, the alternative rule has to be a genuine *alternative*, and not just an additional rule that people could follow in the same circumstances as well.

The second aspect of arbitrariness concerns the nature of reasons for following a convention: The reason for following a rule that is a convention depends on the fact that others follow it too. But we have to be more precise here. There are two possible ways in which the reasons for following a rule are affected by general compliance (in the relevant population), and only one of them is a defining feature of social conventions. The reason for following a rule may sometimes be lost, or seriously compromised, if too many people in the relevant community infringe the rule or otherwise fail to follow it. This, in itself, does not indicate that the rule is arbitrary. Consider, for example, a rule that prohibits smoking in public places. This is not a convention but, let us assume, a rule that is required by the reasons to avoid causing harm to others. Nevertheless, if in a certain place nobody follows the rule and the vicinity is filled with smoke anyway, the reason for following the no-smoking rule is lost. More accurately, we should say that the reason is still there, but it is not an operative reason under the circumstances.[11] Practice-

---

[10] I realize that this is not uncontroversial. For example, Bruno Verbeek in a recent article ("Conventions and Moral Norms") argues that moral norms are conventional. So perhaps no example is free of controversies.

[11] I am assuming here that the room is so smoky that the marginal harm of any additional smoker is basically zero. If you prefer a different example, consider the case of pollution: assume it is wrong to pollute the river, but if the river happens to be so polluted anyway that it makes no difference whether

dependence is a defining feature of conventions, however, only when the fact that others actually follow the rule *initially* forms part of the reasons or the rationale for following it. This is not the case with the no-smoking rule: people should not smoke in public places because it causes harm to others. A certain level of compliance with the rule may be required to ensure its success in solving the problem that the rule is there to solve. But it is not the case that in order to explain what is the point of the no-smoking rule we must appeal to the fact that it happens to be the rule most people follow in the relevant circumstances. Note that I am assuming here that even one smoker in the vicinity of others is causing some harm and that this in itself is a reason to refrain from smoking in the presence of others—unless, that is, the vicinity is so full of smoke anyway that an additional smoker makes no difference. In the case of conventional rules, however, there is a crucial sense in which it is uniquely appropriate to say that we follow the rule partly *because* others follow it too. (We drive on the right side of the road because others drive on it too; or we wear a suit and tie to this party because others will come similarly dressed, etc.)[12]

Let me call this the condition *compliance-dependent reasons*. A reason for following a rule R is compliance dependent if and only if , for a population P in circumstances C,

1. there is a reason for having R, which is also a reason for having at lease one other alternative rule, S, and,

2. part of the reason to follow R instead of S (in circumstances C) consists in the fact that R is the rule actually followed by most members of P in circumstances C. In other words, there is a reason for following R if R is generally complied with, and the same reason is a reason for an alternative rule if that alternative is the rule generally complied with.

Arbitrariness, and therefore conventionality, assumes that the relevant reasons for following the rule are compliance dependent

---

we add some or not, then the reason not to pollute is not an operative reason under the circumstances.

[12] Hume suggested a very similar observation; see *Treatise*, 490.

in this sense. A rule is conventional if and only if there is at least one other potential rule that the relevant community could have followed instead, achieving the same purpose, as it were. The reason for following a convention partly depends on the fact that it just happens to be the rule that people in the relevant community actually follow. Had they followed an alternative rule, the same reason, A, would provide a sufficient reason to follow the alternative rule, namely, the one that people actually follow.

The notion of "sufficient reason" calls for a clarification. Some philosophers may believe that all reasons for action, as such, are sufficient reasons, in that other things being equal, one's failure to act on a reason that applies to the circumstances is, *ipso facto*, wrong. I do not think that this is a correct view of reasons for action. A person may have a reason to play chess, for instance, but it would not be wrong in any sense if she decides not to play chess for no reason at all. In any case, it will not be assumed here that failure to act on a reason is, *ipso facto*, wrong. I do mean, however, that if A is a reason for playing the game according to rule R, R is arbitrary if and only if there is at least one other rule, S, so that if the game was actually played in compliance with S, A would provide a sufficient reason (for the same agents, under the same circumstances) to follow S instead of R.[13] All this indicates that *conventionality is relative to reasons*. Given that A is a reason for R, if R is generally complied with, and A would have been a sufficient reason for an alternative rule if that alternative is generally complied with, then R is conventional relative to A. Note that R need not be conventional altogether, as there may be some other reasons to comply with R that are not convention-type reasons. A norm would be purely conventional, however, if there are no such other reasons.

You may think that all this talk about arbitrariness of conventional norms has not yet been proved; I have not provided any argument to support the assumption here that arbitrariness, as defined above, is an essential feature of conventions. I doubt, however, that any straightforward argument is available.

---

[13] There is a sense, of course, in which it might not be the same game. I will elaborate on some of the difficulties about identity of practices in chapter 2.

My assumption here is that the way we characterized conventional norms captures some basic intuitions we have about such norms, most importantly, the intuition that if a norm is conventional, we could have had a different, alternative, norm that would have served us just as well (in the same circumstances, of course). I have tried to offer a detailed formulation of this intuition; but the formulation cannot be vindicated by an argument. Its validity depends on how theoretically fruitful the formulation is, on how it is put to work in the rest of the argument. In particular, we will have to see how arbitrariness (and compliance dependence) help to clarify not just whether certain types of norm are conventional or not, but also why would it matter that they are, and how could it be philosophically controversial. I believe that defining conventionality in terms that are relative to reasons is going to be helpful in these respects. But of course, whether it is really helpful and to what extent, depends on of the arguments that will be deployed in the rest of this book.

As a final clarification of the definition of conventionality, we need to say something about the idea of rules. Conventions, I have claimed, are social rules. Rules should be distinguished from both regularities of behavior and from generally recognized reasons. Not everything we do regularly we do as an instance of *following a rule*. People regularly eat breakfast, but eating breakfast is not an instance of following a rule. It is just something we tend to do regularly. Rules are normative; the validity of a given rule that applies to the circumstances is a factor in practical reasoning. I will assume here that a rule of conduct exists when there is a certain population[14] that regards the rule as binding. (Needless to say, not every rule that is *regarded* as binding is binding or valid; it is, if there is an adequate reason that supports it.) Without an attempt to define what rules are, we can say at least this: The basic function of rules of conduct is to *replace* (at least some of the) first-order reasons for action. When we make it a rule to φ under circumstances C, it is as if we have made a decision that under circumstances C there is no

---

[14] In some cases, the relevant population can be a single-member set. People can make rules for themselves.

need to deliberate, or to try to figure out, whether to φ or not (that is, up to a point, of course, and under certain conditions, etc.).[15] The rule replaces the need for separate deliberation in each and every context of its application. We take the fact that there is a rule to count in favor of doing φ. In this sense, we take the rule to be binding, namely, we take it as a *pro tanto* reason for action. A regularity of behavior, as such, does not have such normative significance. Consider John who tends to skip breakfast: perhaps it is not wise, and he may be criticized for not being responsive to reasons (assuming there are reasons to eat breakfast), but John could not be sensibly criticized for breaking a rule. There is simply no such a rule.[16] There are many things we have reason to do with some regularity because the circumstances that give rise to the reasons appear in some regular fashion. This, in itself, does not make our conformity with those reasons instances of following a rule. The normativity of rules consists in the fact that the rule, as such, forms part of one's practical reasoning; if the rule is sound, or valid, its application to the circumstances is a fact that counts in favor (or against) doing (or not doing) something.[17]

Rules should also be distinguished from generally recognized reasons. Consider, for example, a game, like chess. It is constituted by a set of rules, some of them very explicit and others, perhaps, less so. In playing the game, players follow the rules of chess. And then, additionally, there may also be some strategies that are widely recognized among players as sound strategies. Now those strategies are not necessarily rules. They might be reasons that apply to some aspect of playing the game, and they may well be widely recognized as such.[18] Admittedly, such strategies can be formulated as rules. When instructing a novice player how to play, one can say, "Don't ever move the king when . . ."; and this sounds very much like a rule. But the

---

[15] See Raz, *Practical Reasons and Norms*.

[16] Unless, of course, John made it a rule to himself to eat breakfast. I am assuming here that this is not the case.

[17] See Hart, *The Concept of Law*, chap. 5.

[18] The distinction, as well as the game example, has been proposed by Warnock, *The Object of Morality*, 45–46.

formulation is potentially misleading. When you point to a rule of the game, you cite the existence of the rule as the reason for action. ("You may only move the bishop diagonally"; "Why?" *"Because* this is the rule.") When you point out a sound strategy, you are not entitled to point to a rule as the relevant reason for action. You just sum up the reasons that apply independently, in a rule-like formulation. Once again, failing to abide by a sound strategy can be criticized as foolish or wrong, but not as breaking a rule. To miss this point is to miss the normative significance of conventions. Conventions are rules of conduct, and they are normatively significant as such.

At one point Lewis raised some doubts about this, arguing that conventions need not necessarily be rules. In many games, he claims, players normally develop a set of tacit and informal understandings about what they are entitled to do in circumstances that are not covered by the rules of the game. These conventions, he contends, are ones left open by the "listed rules" of the game. Lewis concedes that "we might call these understandings rules—unwritten rules, informal rules—if we like." But, he claims, "we would also be inclined to emphasize their differences from the listed rules by saying that they are not rules, but only conventions."[19]

These cryptic remarks are very misleading. For one, they seem to suggest that our concept of a rule ties rules to some sort of formality, as if rules are only those things one would find in rule-books, enlisted and codified systematically, as it were. There is no good reason to hold such a formalistic conception of rules. It is a convention of many games, for instance, that the participants ought to make their moves within a reasonable period of time. As procrastination and lengthy delays would defeat the purpose or the enjoyment of such games, these conventions are often taken for granted and hence left unstated, as it were, by the listed rules of the game. They would normally surface once there is some tendency to deviate from them, and then they might get enlisted and codified like any other rule

---

[19] Lewis, *Convention*, 104–5; a similar view is expressed by Searle, *Construction of Social Reality*, 28.

of the game. Whether codified or not, however, such conventions are certainly part of the rules of the game. In other words, whatever rules are, they are not necessarily "formal," written somewhere, or explicitly promulgated as such.

Second, Lewis's remarks here seem to conflate unlisted rules with generally recognized reasons. "Tacit understandings" that evolve in playing games can be generally recognized strategies that apply, not necessarily rules. To count as rules or conventions, they would have to attain a normative significance. We should be able to say that by not making such and such a move, the player has broken a rule and *thus* did something impermissible. Whether this necessarily calls for a sanction is, of course a separate question. But it is worth noting that typically breaking a rule, as such, can be cited as an adequate justification for a sanction, whereas a failure to abide by a sound strategy cannot.

Lewis is quite right to complain that it is very difficult to define what rules, in the relevant sense, are, and that "the class of so-called rules is a miscellany, with many debatable members."[20] However, it is not a precise definition of rules that we need here. What we need is just to avoid a confusion. And the confusion is to conflate instances of following rules, with mere regularities of behavior or with cases of abiding by a generally recognized reason. It is important to avoid this confusion in order to be able to appreciate the normative significance of social conventions. Conventions, *qua* social rules, are normatively significant. They are cited as reasons for action, and it is precisely the challenge of a theory of conventions to explain what kind of reasons they are.[21] Furthermore, by downplaying this normative significance of conventions as a species of rules, Lewis has opened himself to the criticism that his own account of conventions, which heavily relies on the fact that conventions involve compliance-dependent reasons, is wrong. If we allow generally recognized reasons that are not rules to be examples

---

[20] Lewis, *Convention*, 105.

[21] It seems that in "Languages and Language" Lewis modified his views about this, and basically acknowledged that conventions are essentially normative.

of conventions, it is all too easy to show that conventions need not be practiced in order to exist. If R' is a reason that applies to circumstances C, and is widely recognized as such, R' can be thought to be a convention even if most people in the relevant community fail to follow R' in circumstances C.[22] But this is misguided. It is true of generally recognized reasons, but not of conventions, that they exist regardless of practice. Nothing in the logic of generally recognized reasons requires those reasons to be compliance dependent. One way to block this misguided criticism, then, is by keeping in mind that generally recognized reasons are not conventions.

A possible objection needs to be answered. It might be thought that *beliefs* can be conventional as well, not just rules. For example, people in a certain community may widely share the belief that women should not wear pants; or they may share the belief that it is better to sleep in beds than in hammocks. Countless such beliefs are conventional, according to this line of thought, simply in the sense that they are widely shared in a certain community, and held as the beliefs they are, mostly because they are just widely shared. Now, if beliefs can be conventional, then a widely shared belief in the reasons that apply to certain actions might be conventional as well. And then it is no longer true that conventions can be distinguished from generally recognized reasons.

The problem with this argument lies in its assumption: beliefs are not appropriate candidates for conventionality. Whereas it makes perfect sense, under certain circumstances, to act in a certain way only because others act in the same way (e.g., on which side of the road to drive), it makes no sense to believe that P only because others believe it too. We cannot provide any sensible rationale for conventionality of beliefs, as opposed

---

[22] Indeed, many of Gilbert's counterexamples to Lewis's analysis involve precisely this mistake. The examples she gives are cases of generally recognized reasons, not rules. Hence it is all too easy for her to argue that their existence does not depend on general compliance; see *On Social Facts*, 344–55. My remarks here are also meant to apply to Millikan's view (see her "Conventions of Language Made Simple," 173–74, and, more generally, her *Language: A Biological Model*).

to rules that guide action. It is true, of course, that we often come to have beliefs, that is, we acquire them, because we get a sense that others in our vicinity have those beliefs and perhaps hold them strongly. This may be a fact about our psychology, but it is beside the point. In justifying a belief he holds, a person would make a fool of himself by saying, "I believe that P because everybody else does."²³ Beliefs are appraised by their truth or falsehood, not by their compliance with others' beliefs. In other words, whereas we may have compliance-dependent reasons (for action), something like compliance-dependent belief is not a coherent idea. There is no case in which it is true that (1) X believes that P and (2) had it been the case that everybody else believed that not-P, X would have had a *sufficient reason* to believe that not-P. So what about the examples? Is there no sense in which we can properly speak about conventionally held beliefs? Perhaps there is, in a derivative or metaphorical sense. We can talk about conventional beliefs when we want to indicate that the belief in question is not warranted by its truth, but is widely held nevertheless. Or perhaps when we intend to indicate that the belief represents a traditional way of thought, reflecting a social custom, or such. Either way, the notion of convention is used imperfectly here, and does not withstand philosophical analysis. Conventions are social rules that purport to guide action; they are not beliefs.

A final question before we turn to Lewis's theory. One may wonder whether there are *social* norms that are not conventions. Is the category of social norms wider than that of social conventions? Now of course, this very much depends on how we understand the idea of social norms. But let us assume a simple, intuitive understanding here, whereby social norms are simply those norms that are widely followed in a certain community, and they do not originate in any institutional enact-

---

²³ Unless one has independent reasons for thinking that a certain population is more likely to have correct beliefs on a particular issue. I can justify my beliefs on certain scientific matters by citing the fact that those in a position to know such things hold those beliefs. In this sense, I use others' beliefs as a kind of indication or evidence for truth. But none of this would show that beliefs can be conventional.

ment (like legal norms or regulations of a college, etc.). So the question is, are all social norms necessarily conventions? I think that the answer is no, because many of the social norms we follow are not arbitrary in the sense defined above. Some social norms do not have genuine alternatives that we could have followed instead without a significant loss in their purpose or function. Consider, for example, cultures in which it is a widely accepted social norm that younger people should care for the elderly. Presumably, this is a morally sound norm that is supported by good reasons, and those reasons are not compliance dependent. The fact that the norm happens to be socially accepted and followed in the community does not make it conventional. And of course, similar considerations apply to countless other social norms that instantiate sound moral principles. True, it often happens that such norms are actually manifest in a variety of specific norms that are conventional. For example, conventions may determine ways in which care and respect for the elderly is actually instantiated in the relevant community. But the underlying social norm that requires such care and respect remains nonconventional, that is, even when there is a variety of norms that conventionally determine its application. In short, I don't think that we are entitled to assume that all social norms are conventional; each case needs to be examined on its own terms.

David Lewis on Conventions

David Lewis provided an ingenious account of social conventions that, at least in its core, has been widely accepted ever since.[24] Lewis claimed that conventions are social rules that emerge as practical solutions to wide-scale, recurrent, coordination problems. Interestingly, Lewis's account of social conventions was aimed at answering Quine's doubts about the conventionality of language. Quine argued that language cannot be conventional because conventions are essentially

[24] Lewis, *Convention*.

agreements, and of course, we have never agreed with each other to abide by the rules of language. More importantly, we would have needed at least some rudimentary language in which to express the first agreements. Lewis replied that Quine's assumption was simply wrong: conventions do not result from agreements. On the contrary, conventions tend to emerge precisely in those cases where an agreement is very difficult or impossible to reach (because of the large number of people involved, for example), and a solution to a recurrent coordination problem is needed.

A coordination problem arises when several agents have a particular structure of preferences with respect to their mutual modes of conduct: namely, that between several alternatives of conduct open to them in a given set of circumstances, each and every agent has a stronger preference to act in concert with the other agents, than his own preference for acting upon any one of the particular alternatives.[25] Most coordination problems in our lives are easily solved by simple agreements between the agents to act upon one more or less arbitrarily chosen alternative, thus securing concerted action among them. However, when a particular coordination problem is recurrent in a given set of circumstances, and agreement is difficult to obtain (mostly because of the large number of agents involved), a social rule is very likely to emerge, and this rule is a convention. Conventions, in other words, emerge as solutions to large-scale recurrent coordination problems, not as a result of an agreement, but as an alternative to such an agreement, precisely in those cases where agreements are difficult or impossible to obtain.

Lewis's analysis of conventions in terms of solutions to recurrent coordination problems embodies remarkable advantages. Quite apart from the fact that it is capable of explaining the emergence of conventions without relying on the need for agreement, it also explains the essential conditions of conventionality.

---

[25] Lewis defined coordination problems in terms of a standard game-theoretical model. The details of such models have been substantially revised since, and the models game theorists work with have become much more sophisticated. See, for example, Sugden, *Economics of Rights*; Vanderschraaf, "Convention as Correlated Equilibrium"; Bacharach, *Beyond Individual Choice*; Bicchieri, *The Grammar of Society*.

If the whole point of a conventional rule is to secure concerted action among a number of agents in accordance with their own dominant preferences, then it is quite clear why the reasons for following a convention are compliance-dependent reasons. Solving a coordination problem is a paradigmatic example of compliance-dependent reasons: I have a reason to do P (and not Q or R) if, and only if, I have reason to assume that others will do P as well (and not Q or R). And then it also becomes quite clear why it is the case that conventional rules are arbitrary in the requisite sense. Once again, it is the very structure of a coordination problem that there are at least two alternatives of conduct open before the agents in question, and that they have a stronger preference to act in concert than to act upon any other alternative they may (subjectively) prefer. If a given rule is a solution to a coordination problem, then it is already assumed that there is an alternative rule that the agents could have followed instead, solving the relevant coordination problem they had faced.

So far so good. Lewis, however, added another layer to his explanation, concerning the ways in which conventional rules tend to emerge. Following standard game-theoretical analysis (as known at the time), Lewis suggested that when there is a recurrent coordination problem and there are many agents involved, so that agreements are difficult, if not impossible, to reach, people would tend to opt for the option that happens to be salient, assuming that others would opt for the salient option as well, thus securing the relevant concerted action. I am sure that this often happens. I doubt, however, that it is the business of a philosophical analysis to explain how conventions emerge, as a matter of a historical account. I would guess that many of the conventions we follow emerged almost by accident, and many have emerged for various obscure reasons that we can hardly even trace back to their historical origin. (I have heard that the convention of a salute in the army evolved from medieval knights' practice of greeting their opponents by raising the visor of their helmet before battle. Whether this is a true story, I don't know; the point is that there are many like it.)[26]

---

[26] Here's another example: I have heard that the convention to say "hello" when responding to a telephone call comes from Hungarian; the Hungarians

In any case, as long as we understand that large-scale recurrent coordination problems can be solved without the necessity of an agreement between the relevant agents, Lewis's theory proves its point. The suggestion that we tend to follow salient options, and thus solve coordination problems, is one plausible speculation, but not more than this.[27]

Be this as it may, the main problem with Lewis's analysis concerns its scope. It is difficult to deny that many conventions are, indeed, normative solutions to large-scale recurrent coordination problems. Clear examples would be notational conventions, like the sound-sense conventions of languages, early conventions of the road, such as on which side of the road to drive (that is, before such conventions were replaced by legal regulation), and many others. But the mistake here is to generalize from some cases to all. There are important types of social conventions that do not fit this analysis. Generally, the problem is this: Lewis's analysis assumes that *first* there is a recurrent coordination problem in a given set of circumstances, and then a social rule evolves that solves the problem for the relevant agents. For many types of familiar conventions, however, this story does not make sense. Antecedently to the emergence of the convention, there is no coordination problem that we can identify, at least not without already assuming that the conventional practice is in place.[28]

Consider, for example, a structured game, like chess. Presumably, the rules constituting the game of chess are (or at

---

were, they claim, among the first to invent the contraption, concomitantly with Bell and Gray, and the word "hello" is a slight distortion of the Hungarian word "hallod," which literally means "do you hear." Others credit Edison with the introduction of this convention. Who knows? Either way, salience seems to have very little to do with it.

[27] For a much more empirically based account, see, for example, Bicchieri, *The Grammar of Society*, chap. 2.

[28] Several writers have criticized Lewis's generalization in this respect, though mostly on game-theoretical grounds. See, for example, Miller, "Rationalizing Conventions"; Sugden, *Economics of Rights*; and Vanderschraaf, "Convention as Correlated Equilibrium," and see also Davis, *Meaning, Expression, and Thought*. Gilbert and, to some extent, Millikan, reject Lewis's model on other, more general grounds. More on this below.

least were, before institutionally codified) conventions.[29] Does it make sense to suggest that the rules of chess are there to solve a coordination problem between potential chess players? Have these rules evolved as a solution to some large-scale recurrent coordination problem that we could have specified before the emergence of the game itself? I think it is extremely unlikely that playing by the rules of chess solves a coordination problem between the players; as if there had been a coordination problem between potential chess players before chess was invented, as it were, and now they play by the rules to solve that problem. This seems implausible. Of course you can structure a very vague and highly general coordination problem, say, a desire to play some intellectual board game. (Note that even for this general problem to be specified, we would need a fairly elaborate conception of what board games are, which in itself is conventionally determined. But let's ignore this complication for now.) So allegedly, you can say that there was this general coordination problem: there we are, wanting to play some structured board game, and then rules have evolved to solve *that* problem. The obvious difficulty is that such a coordination problem would be too abstract and underspecified. If you allow for almost any concerted action between a number of agents to count as a solution to a coordination problem in the relevant sense, then you will end up with the conclusion that all social interactions are solutions to coordination problems. That seems to be very unlikely and philosophically unhelpful.

More importantly, there is something seriously amiss about the suggestion to characterize the rationale of playing chess as a solution to a coordination problem. When asked, for example, why I drive on the right side of the road, it makes perfect sense to reply that I do it because I need to coordinate my

---

[29] You may have some doubts about the appropriateness of the example. In chapter 2 I explain in greater detail why the rules of chess are conventional, and I also discuss the ways in which conventions tend to be codified and how codification affects the conventionality of the relevant practice. For now, chess is really just one possible example; if you have doubts about the conventionality of chess, think about other cases, like practices of etiquette, various social rituals, conventions of artistic genres (discussed below), etc.

driving with others. But when asked why I play chess right now, it would be perplexing to reply that I do it because I need to coordinate my behavior with my fellow players. There are two related points that I want to make here: first, even if we could tell a story that would explain the *emergence* of chess as a solution to some vague coordination problem, such a story would be quite irrelevant to our present concerns when playing chess. To solve a coordination problem is not why players indulge in this game. In the case of coordination conventions, the reasons for the emergence of the convention and the reasons for complying with the convention in each and every instance, are basically the same: to solve the relevant coordination problem. In the case of a game, like chess, however, this is not necessarily, or even typically, true. The reasons for the emergence of the relevant practice need not be the same as the reasons for complying with its norms on specific occasions. Once the game is there and can be played, it may give reasons for the agents to follow its rules that are quite independent of the story of why and how the game has emerged. (More on this in chapter 2.)

Second, and more important, the reasons people normally have for playing chess have very little to do with solving a coordination problem. Of course, once the game is there and it is being played, it may give rise to various coordination problems that might then get solved by additional rules or conventions. But the essential rationale of the game is ill explained in terms of a solution to a coordination problem. It is true, of course, that in playing any structured game, part of the reason we have to stick to the rules, and be sure that we all know what the rules are, is to make sure that our actions are well coordinated. So yes, undoubtedly there is a coordinative function to any such rule-guided activity, like playing a structured competitive game. But this is only one aspect of playing chess, not its main rationale. And it is an aspect that is present in any rule-governed activity, whether conventional or not.

Consider a different example, from the realm of arts. Most forms of art are at least partly conventional. Conventions determine, for example, what theater is, how it is staged, what one is to expect from such a performance, and so on. Would it make any sense to suggest that conventions constituting such artistic forms or genres are also solutions to coordination problems? Does it make sense to assume that before theater evolved as a specific form of art, there was some recurrent coordination problem that needed to be solved, and then the conventions of theater evolved to solve it? What would that coordination problem be, and for whom? So I hope you see where I am heading here: either we construe the idea of a coordination problem in such abstract and general terms as to be completely unhelpful, or else we must give up the idea that all social conventions are explicable in terms of solutions to recurrent coordination problems. The latter option should be easy to follow. Social conventions evolve as responses to numerous kinds of social needs, they serve a wide variety of social functions, and we have no reason to assume that all those needs are reducible to coordination problems. This idea will be further developed in the next chapter.

An Alternative Account?

The details of Lewis's theory of conventions have been criticized by many philosophers, but few have suggested an entirely different approach.[30] Margaret Gilbert's work is a notable exception: she has argued for an alternative account of what social conventions are, one that is quite different from Lewis's. The gist of Gilbert's characterization of social conventions is the following:

[30] See note 28 above. How to classify, in this respect, Millikan's account of conventions as patterns of behavior sustained by weight of precedent, is something that I find very difficult to determine. On the one hand, she seems to share some of Lewis's basic insights about the nature of conventionality; in particular, she quite explicitly endorses Lewis's account of arbitrariness (see her "Conventions of Language Made Simple," 167). On the other hand, her account deviates from Lewis's in many crucial points, some of which are at odds with my suggestions here (e.g., that conventions are necessarily rules/norms), while others not necessarily. Be this as it may, the main difference between the account I offer here and Millikan's view consists in the relation of conventions to reasons. On my view, conventionality is relative to reasons; on her view, conventions have basically nothing to do with reasons.

[O]ur everyday concept of a social convention is that of a jointly accepted principle of action, a group fiat with respect to how one is to act in certain situations. . . . conventions on this account are essentially collectivity-involving: a population that develops a convention in this sense becomes by that very fact a collectivity. Further, each party to the convention will accept that each one personally ought to conform, other things being equal, where the "ought" is understood to be based on the fact that together they jointly accept the principle.[31]

Before we try to untangle some of these concepts, a few points have to be mentioned. First, as we have already noted, Gilbert explicitly rejects the assumption that conventions have to be practiced by a certain community in order to exist as social conventions. Second, and more problematically, Gilbert explicitly rejects the idea that arbitrariness is an essential characterization of conventional norms. The problem is, however, that Gilbert explicitly assumes that Lewis's definition of arbitrariness is equivalent to indifference.[32] Since we have already seen in some detail that indifference is not what is entailed by an appropriate definition of the arbitrariness of conventions, Gilbert's criticism misses its target here. Furthermore, failing to realize the essentially arbitrary nature of conventions results in the failure to see that the reasons for following conventions are compliance-dependent reasons. And then it becomes very doubtful that it is really "our everyday concept of a social convention" that Gilbert is explicating here.

Be this as it may, there are two main concepts in her characterization of conventions worth looking at. First, Gilbert defines conventions in terms of a "group fiat" or of a "jointly accepted principle of action." Second, she claims that conventions are "essentially collectivity-involving: a population that develops a convention in this sense becomes by that very fact a collectivity." I think that both concepts are misguided. The latter is really just a generalization from some (very few, actually)

31 *On Social Facts*, 377.
32 Ibid., 341.

cases to all, and the former confuses conventions with generally recognized reasons or, alternatively, agreements. Let me take up these points in this reversed order.

It is true that the acceptance of certain social norms is sometimes constitutive of a group identity. One becomes a football fan, for example, by, *inter alia*, accepting the norms that govern this practice. The group's adherence to such norms is partly what defines the identity of the group. Are such norms that constitute group identity necessarily conventions? Probably not. To take an extreme example, some philosophers suggest that our adherence to norms of rationality and practical reasoning is what defines or constitutes our humanity. Surely this is not a matter of convention. Or think about the common suggestion that American (that is, U.S.) identity is partly constituted by accepting certain principles of political morality, like cherishing individual freedom, free enterprise, constitutional protection of civil rights, and so on. In short, it seems that "essentially collectivity-involving" norms need not be conventions. More importantly, however, conventions need not be collectivity-involving. Some conventions are, but many conventions have no such role to play. There are numerous conventions we follow that have nothing to do with group identity. Consider, for example, something like the notational convention of the arrow sign. As far as I know, in most cultures the sign of an arrow is a conventional means of pointing to a certain direction in space. Does it make any sense to suggest that by following the arrow convention all of us become a collectivity? What collectivity would that be? And do we become a collectivity by following conventions of the road, or notational conventions of a language, and so on? The connection between conventions and group identity is contingent, at best. This collectivity involving feature is not a defining feature of social conventions.

The concept of "group fiat" or "jointly accepted principle of action" is also very problematic. To begin with, it might be overinclusive. A principle of action that is jointly accepted can be an instance of a generally recognized reason for action, or some other type of social norm, not necessarily a convention. Suppose, for example, that it is a "jointly accepted principle of action" in my department that we do not burden our junior faculty with committee assignments. This is not necessarily a convention. More plausibly, it is a principle of action we adhere to because we recognize it to be a good practice. We generally recognize that it is better for the junior faculty to be able to focus on their research and teaching until they acquire more experience, and we try to implement this principle by excluding them from administrative work. Perhaps we regard it as a "group fiat" or a "jointly accepted principle," but this would not make it a convention. Generally speaking, how people see themselves committed to a given norm does not entail anything about the kind of norm it is.

Gilbert would reply that I have missed a crucial point here about the idea of a joint acceptance. Presumably, what she means is some notion of *conditional* acceptance based on reciprocity: I commit myself to N if and only if you commit yourself too, and you commit yourself to N if and only if I do. If something like this is what Gilbert has in mind, then perhaps the above example is not a counterexample. But then two other problems emerge: first, this notion of joint acceptance as conditional on reciprocity would seem to be inconsistent with some of Gilbert's critical remarks about Lewis's account. Second, and more important, it is very difficult to make sense of the idea of conditional acceptance without relying on the idea of agreement. Let me explain.

One of Gilbert's main criticisms of Lewis's account of conventions consists in her claim that conventions are not based on what I have called compliance-dependent reasons. As she put it: "social conventions can exist in the absence of expectations of conformity."[33] But then, if you do not need to expect general conformity, what could you mean by "joint acceptance" as a reciprocal condition? I accept N only if you accept it too, but I do not need to expect you to comply with N? That is a strange form of reasoning. In other words, if conventions do not have to involve compliance-dependent reasons, then the idea of reciprocity cannot be rationalized either.

<hr>

[33] Ibid., at 348.

More importantly, however, the idea of joint acceptance construed in this conditional way would seem to require some notion of agreement to give it any hold in reality. Conditional acceptance, in this sense, is precisely the rationale of a contract: I accept the terms only if you do, and vice versa, you would accept if I do. Gilbert is aware of this. Conventions, she says, are norms of *quasi*-agreement. Now the need for the "quasi" qualifier is clear enough: as Quine and Lewis rightly observed, there is no hope for any account of the conventionality of language if we have to assume that conventions emerge from agreements. So if we are back to the agreement requirement, it better not be anything like an explicit agreement. Hence the suggestion that conventions are *quasi*-agreements. The difficulty, of course, is to provide this "quasi" qualifier with any concrete substance in this context. I don't see how it can be done.

In numerous contexts and for different reasons, philosophers have tried to rely on the idea that there are cases that are like an agreement, but without the explicit speech acts that would normally constitute an agreement. For example, we can have agreement by some other speech act equivalent, such as a body movement or an inference from some particular behavior. This is still an explicit form of agreement and one that is parasitic on the standard speech act cases. If this is what is meant by "quasi-agreement," Quine's problem remains.

Gilbert seems to agree, since she characterizes quasi-agreement as a situation in which no agreement of any kind had taken place, but the situation is one in which "it is as if they have agreed."[34] What are we to make of this? There are two possibilities to make sense of such a locution, but none of them would be helpful. On one possible reading, something may look as if it resulted from an agreement if it is an instance of an invisible-hand mechanism. Those are cases in which people's behavior over time *looks like* conduct that has emerged from concerted, purposeful, action, when in fact, it has not. This familiar invisible-hand mechanism would not help Gilbert's account, however, since it explicitly denies precisely what Gilbert

---

[34] Ibid., at 369.

needs here, namely, the idea of some reciprocity, or conditional acceptance. (Note that it is a crucial aspect of an invisible-hand mechanism that the agents act independently of each other, pursuing her own individual ends.)

The second way in which we can make sense of the idea that there are situations that we can treat *as if* there was an agreement is a moral construal. Sometimes we think that people are under an obligation to φ even in the absence of an agreement (or consent) on their part to φ, because we are entitled to treat them as if they had agreed to φ. What those situations are, and how to explain this kind of justification, is a familiar and daunting challenge to many moral philosophers, but we need not go into this here. What Gilbert needs in order to substantiate the idea of a quasi-agreement is not this kind of moral justification. The question we face is not how to justify, morally, a requirement of compliance with norms that do not emerge from agreements. We need an account of what such norms *are*. So here is what Gilbert's account needs: how to explain, without relying on the idea of an agreement, a situation in which the basic rationale of a given social norm is that I will do φ only if you φ, and vice versa, you will φ only if I do. We know one way in which it works: this is a standard coordination problem. So it seems that we have not avoided Lewis's analysis after all. At least not on Gilbert's account. What we need is a fresh start. We need an account of the rationale of those conventions that does not consist in a solution to coordination problems. I propose such an account in the next chapter.

CHAPTER TWO

Constitutive Conventions

In the previous chapter we have seen that Lewis's analysis of social conventions in terms of solutions to large-scale recurrent coordination problems successfully explains some cases, but not others. There is a whole range of social conventions that cannot be explained in terms of a solution to coordination problems. In this chapter I want to develop the idea that there is a second type of social conventions, whose main function is to constitute social practices. I call them *constitutive conventions*. I will try to explain what constitutive conventions are and how they differ from coordination conventions.

REGULATIVE AND CONSTITUTIVE RULES

There are countless social activities that are constituted by rules. To mention but a few familiar examples, consider structured games, like chess or football, forms of art, like theater, poetry, or symphonic music, social ceremonies, like a wedding or an initiation ritual and, of course, certain aspects of language use. I will assume that it is not controversial that such practices are, to a considerable extent, rule governed, and that the rules in question play a certain constitutive function. The purpose of this chapter is to explore what this constitutive relation consists in, and how it helps to explain the nature of conventions that constitute social practices.

It might be useful to begin with the distinction between regulative and constitutive rules suggested by John Searle. As he
defined the distinction, "regulative rules regulate antecedently
or independently existing forms of behavior; . . . constitutive
rules do not merely regulate, they create or define new forms
of behavior."[1] Now, it would be natural to suggest that this
distinction corresponds to the distinction between coordination conventions, which are regulative rules, and constitutive
conventions. Though this is basically the line that I will pursue
here, Searle's distinction is in need of some modifications.

Searle was aware of an obvious difficulty with the distinction:
one can say that every rule is constitutive of a new mode of conduct, namely, that of following the rule on its occasions of application. Every rule is constitutive of the practice of following
it, as it were. Since every constitutive rule would also regulate
behavior, one might suspect that the distinction is really just a
distinction between two different functions that rules have, that
of regulating behavior and thus also, of constituting modes of
behavior as instances of following the rule.[2] I think that Searle
had anticipated this objection and, in response, made the following observation:

> Where the rule is purely regulative, behavior which is in ac-
> cordance with the rule could be given the same description or
> specification (the same answer to the question "What did he
> do?") whether or not the rule existed, provided the description
> or specification makes no explicit reference to the rule. But where
> the rule (or system of rules) is constitutive, behavior which is in
> accordance with the rule can receive specifications or descriptions
> which it could not receive if the rule or rules did not exist.[3]

Consider, for example, the rule that regulates on which side of
the road to drive. We can easily specify the conduct of the agent
without invoking the relevant rule. An answer to the question
What does he do? can be given—he drives on the right side of the

[1] *Speech Acts*, 33
[2] This is the gist of the criticism mentioned by Warnock in *The Object of
Morality*, 37–38. See also Raz, *Practical Reason and Norms*, at 109.
[3] *Speech Acts*, 35

road—without any implicit reference to the rule that prescribes this mode of behavior. On the other hand, consider locutions like "X *appointed* Y to chair the committee"; "X *scored checkmate* in just fifteen moves"; "X *performed* Hamlet . . ." In all these and similar cases, the relevant conduct cannot be understood or fully specified as the kind of conduct that it is, without the invocation of the set of rules that constitute the practice within which such conduct or locution is performed. A description of the relevant action italicized in the examples above without the rules, and their description in the context of the rules, is markedly different. Searle further suggested that regulative rules typically take a certain conduct or behavior as their object, like "Do X" or "If you do X, then Y . . ." Whereas constitutive rules typically have the form of "X counts as Y" or "X counts as Y in context C."[4]

Both of these characterizations of the distinction are somewhat rough and inaccurate. Consider, for example, the rule that requires standing in line for some event, like purchasing a ticket at the cinema. Now the problem is that according to Searle's formulation, the rule might come out as a constitutive one: a specification of the action without invoking the rule is quite different from its specification as an instance of following the rule. "He is standing there behind X in front of Y" doesn't quite capture what is going on. "He is standing there in line for . . . ," on the other hand, seems to invoke the rule-governed practice of standing in line. But the rule does not seem to be constitutive. It simply regulates a certain mode of behavior, just like the driving on the right side of the road rule. Similar problems occur with the second criterion, or indicator. Some regulative rules can take the form of "P counts as Q (in context C)." For example, we can instruct our students that sending an essay assignment by email counts as (or does not count as) timely submission. This is a regulative rule, if anything is. It just prescribes to the students how they may, or may not, submit their assignments. The locution "P counts as Q" is neither here nor there.[5]

4 Ibid., 34–35.

5 Later, in his *Social Construction of Reality*, Searle uses this formula in a much deeper sense, generally representing the sense in which brute facts are assigned institutional significance by collective intentionality. My concerns in this book

Some distinctions may be quite intuitive, even if difficult to define precisely. But it is worth exploring what gives rise to the difficulty. Perhaps it is this: Rules do not, strictly speaking, constitute behavior or conduct. Rules can prescribe a certain conduct, permit or prohibit a certain form of behavior, and the like. What seems to be constituted by rules, in the relevant cases, is not the agents' actions or behavior, but the particular social meaning or significance of the action in question. Thus when Searle suggests that sometimes we cannot fully specify the agent's action without invoking the relevant rules, what he probably means is that we cannot specify the social meaning of the conduct without taking into account the rules that confer on it the meaning it has in the relevant context. Undoubtedly, there is something true about this. But it is doubtful that this clarification would suffice to clarify the distinction between regulative and constitutive rules. There is a sense in which every instance of *following a rule*, as such, might gain its social meaning only as such an instance of following a rule. There is, after all, a difference between driving on the right side of the road, and doing the same thing while complying with a general rule that requires it. So it seems that every social rule constitutes, to some extent, the specific social meaning or significance of instances of following it.

In spite of these difficulties, I think that Searle's insight is basically correct and captures something of great importance. If there was a mistake here, it was to assume that rules constitute particular actions or "new forms of behavior."[6] Actions are not constituted by rules, but social practices, that is, certain types of *activities*, are. It is only when we have a whole structure of rule-governed activity, with some complexity and interconnections between the rules, that we can say that we have a social

---

are not about the metaphysics of social reality, and my comments are not meant to apply to Searle's thesis in this metaphysical context.

[6] I am actually not so sure that Searle made such an assumption; he formulated the distinction in such a way as to give the impressing that he is talking about a constitutive relation between rules and actions. However, his emphasis on the systematic nature of constitutive rules makes me think that he would have agreed with the reformulations suggested here.

practice constituted by rules. So let me suggest that constitutive rules are those rules that constitute a type of activity, a social practice. Therefore, I will concentrate on social practices and the ways in which such practices are constituted by rules or conventions. There are two main types of such constitutive rules: social conventions and institutionally enacted rules.[7] In other words, social practices can be of two main types: conventional or institutional. As we shall see later in the chapter, sometimes conventional practices are replaced by institutional codification, and thus they may become institutional practices.[8] Let me give some examples of conventional and of institutional practices:

Examples of conventional practices:

1. Structured conventional games (like chess, tennis, soccer, etc.)
2. Forms of art (and some genres) (like theater, opera, poetry, etc.)
3. (Some) practices of etiquette (like table manners, greeting conventions, linguistic forms of addressing different types of subjects, etc.)
4. Social ceremonies and rituals (like weddings, prom parties, etc.)

Examples of institutional practices:

1. Legal institutions (like legislatures, courts, administrative agencies, etc.)
2. Quasi-legal (or derivative) institutions (like a college or a university, political parties, clubs of various kinds, sports leagues, etc.)[9]
3. Religious institutions (like a church, a congregation, etc.)

---

[7] In fact, there is probably a third type of constitutive rules, which I will largely ignore here: one can construct an artificial "game," as it were, by laying out a set of rules that constitute the activity. Many nonconventional games are like that. One just "enacts," as it were, a set of rules that constitute the game (like solitaire, and nowadays, countless computer games). These games do not necessarily form social practices, though they may become social practices under certain conditions.

[8] Notably, Searle explicitly denies that constitutive rules can be conventions. See his *Construction of Social Reality*, 28. He provides no arguments for this conclusion, nor for the distinction he draws there between rules and conventions.

[9] These institutions are not legal, in the sense of being part of the law, but they are legally authorized and regulated.

Naturally, my purpose here is to concentrate on conventional practices. I will argue that such practices are constituted by social conventions of a special type, quite distinct from coordination conventions.

CONSTITUTIVE CONVENTIONS AND VALUES

Needless to say, the idea of a social practice is rather vague and overinclusive. Many things can be called a social practice, and not all of them are relevant for our discussion. I will use the term "social practice" in a specific sense, and I will try to clarify and narrow it down as we go along. Chess would be a good example to work with. It is a fairly well defined social practice, constituted by conventional rules. As we have noted in the previous chapter, the rules constituting chess cannot be explicated in terms of Lewis-type coordination conventions. The rules constituting chess are *constitutive conventions*. Their function is to define what the game is and how to play it: the conventions define what counts as winning and losing a game, what are permissible and impermissible moves in the game, and so on. Note that constitutive conventions always have a dual function: the rules both constitute the practice, and, at the same time, they regulate conduct within it.[10]

Furthermore, and I will argue that this is typical, the constitutive conventions of chess at least partly define, or constitute, some of the values we associate with the game and a whole range of evaluative discourse that appropriately applies to it. To begin with, the rules constitute chess as a competitive game that one can win or lose; and the rules are such that they constitute a particular kind of competition between the players that is, basically, the point or purpose of indulging in the game. It is the kind a competition that values certain intellectual skills of strategic computation, memory, and such. In fact, it is more subtle than this; skilled players would have a pretty clear sense

---

[10] This dual function of constitutive rules was noted by Searle, *Speech Acts*, 33.

of what counts as an elegant move or sloppy one, a brilliant strategy as opposed to a reckless one, and so on.

That there are certain values constituted by the rule of chess can be seen quite clearly, I believe, if we imagine a different kind of chess, so to speak, with some different rules. Imagine, for example, a game like chess that is designed in such a way as to last indefinitely, without the possibility of winning it; or imagine a similar game that would also allow players to intimidate their opponents by threatening with use of some physical force; surely, these games would have established rather different kinds of values than the ones we associate with chess as we know it.

This is quite generally the case. When conventions constitute a social practice, they typically constitute some of the values that are inherent in the practice and the kind of evaluative discourse that applies to it. More precisely, *following* constitutive conventions amounts to a type of activity, and it is this activity that has value for those who engage in it (and sometimes others who care about it). Some of these values, however, are such that they only make sense as instances of following the relevant conventions; we can only explain the value they have in the specific context, and on the background of, the practice that is constituted by the conventions.

Consider, as another example, forms of art, like theater or opera. The conventions that constitute such genres also determine, to a considerable extent, the particular values of the genre, and the evaluative discourse that is deemed appropriate to apply to it. Many of the values we may find in, say, theater, are not necessarily unique to this genre. But some of them certainly are. There are certain theatrical-dramatic values and standards of appraisal that are unique to theater; they are partly constituted by the conventions of this genre. The conventions that constitute the theatrical genre(s) determine, to some extent, what it is that makes sense to say about theater, and what wouldn't make sense to say about it. It makes sense to talk about the dramatic aspects of a theatrical performance, but not about its competitiveness or strategic computation. And this is because the conventions of theater are such that they define

certain criteria of success or excellence in that practice, criteria
that would be very difficult to grasp without understanding the
conventions, and their emergent practice.[11]

Admittedly, it is not easy to distinguish between values that
are constituted by the relevant conventions and values that we
associate with an activity just by grasping the nature of the activity and the kind of thing that it is. The fact that we associate
certain norms of rationality, for example, with the activity of
providing an argument, does not indicate that such norms are
constituted by rules or conventions. We can only say that a
certain evaluation is (partly) constituted by conventions if it is
the case that we could not have grasped or come to appreciate
the relevant value without understanding the conventions that
constitute the relevant practice.

One might object that values are just not the kind of things
that can be constituted by rules, conventional or other.[12] Following a rule R under circumstances C might be valuable, or
not, but the rule itself cannot constitute its value. Now, I think
that this is correct, but it doesn't undermine my point about
constitutive conventions. We have to be very careful about the
way in which we characterize the relations between constitutive
conventions and values. Strictly speaking, a rule cannot constitute a value, just as it cannot constitute an action. Rules guide
actions in various ways, and in a systematic structure they can
constitute a social practice. It is the practice of following the
rules that has value for those who engage in it. Consider (yet
again) the rules of chess. None of those rules that constitute
chess, taken one by one, as it were, can be said to constitute
a value. The game, however, is valuable for those who play it
(and presumably those who enjoy watching it, etc.). And this
is in accord with the truth that what is valuable is *following* the
rule(s) under the circumstances. The question is how exactly to

[11] I think that this idea is implicit in McIntyre's discussion of "internal
goods" of social practices; see *After Virtue*, 187–89.
[12] Some versions of constructivism in ethics might not find a problem here
at all. A discussion of constructivism as a metaethical stance would go far beyond the confines of this chapter.

define the relation of "constitution" between the conventions that constitute the practice and some of the values of the practice. Let me suggest that there are two possibilities here: there is a weak and a stronger sense of constituting values, and they are not mutually exclusive.

On the weaker sense of constituting value, we would say that the value of following R under circumstances C is contingent on the fact that R forms *part of a system* of rules, S, that constitute a (presumably valuable) practice. In other words, following R is valuable *only in the context of S*. For example, there is nothing valuable in following the rule that requires moving the bishop diagonally; it is only valuable to follow this rule in the context of playing chess, as a whole game, so to speak. I take it that this is neither controversial, nor unique to the context of our discussion here.

There is, however, a stronger sense in which rules constituting a practice also constitute some of its values. We could say that a system of rules, S, constitutes a value in the strong sense, if it is the case that engaging in the practice constituted by S is valuable (at least for those who engage in it) in ways in which it *could not have been valuable without the existence of S*. In other words, but for the existence of the constitutive conventions of S, the relevant value could not have materialized. So the idea here is that there are certain values of, say, theatrical performance, that could not have been present without the existence of the conventional genre of theater; or certain values of poetic excellence could not have been realized without the relevant genres of poetry in existence. And the same goes for appreciation of strategic computation in chess, and perhaps even certain manifestations of civility that are only created by existing practices of etiquette.

Now, this formulation still leaves an ambiguity between an epistemic version of it and an ontological one. It is possible to claim that a social practice enables us to realize or appreciate values that we could not have otherwise come to appreciate or, in an ontological sense, that the practice actually creates values that otherwise could not have existed without it. I think that the latter is possible, but there is no need for substantiating this here. The epistemic version is quite sufficient. Even if it is the

case that social practices only enable us to appreciate values that
otherwise we could not have come to appreciate, the main thesis
about the relation between constitutive conventions and values
remains. The further question of whether the constituted values
could have somehow *existed* even without the conventional
practice is a difficult question about the ontology of values that
I need not resolve here.

Another point needs to be observed. Generally, it would be
a mistake to equate a social practice with the rules or conventions that constitute it. There is typically much more to a social
practice than following its constitutive rules. People can follow
the rules of chess, for example, but just pretend to play chess,
or they can follow the rules while believing that it is all part of
an elaborate religious ritual, and then perhaps they would not
be *playing chess*. To be sure, I do not want to deny that the game
is made possible by following its rules. On the contrary, as I
have tried to suggest, the rules actually constitute the practice.
But they do not exhaust it. The relations between the rules and
their emergent social practice is not one of identity. There is
no practice without the rules, and if the rules were different the
practice would have been different as well, but there is more to
the practice then just following its rules.[13]

At least part of the explanation for this nonidentity relation
consists in the complex social functions and needs that constitutive conventions tend to respond to. Chess has not evolved to
solve a particular problem that we could identify antecedently
and independently of the game itself, and of the more general
human activity of playing competitive games. Chess can only be
understood on the background of understanding a whole range
of social needs and various aspects of human nature, such as our
need to play games, to win, to be intellectually challenged, to
be able to understand a distinction between real-life concerns
and "artificial" or "detached" structures of interaction, and so
forth. In other words, there are always some reasons, functions,
needs, and the like, at the background of social practices, and
those reasons are typically instantiated by the conventions that

---

[13] See Schwyzer, "Rules and Practices."

constitute the practice. And then, once a conventional practice is in play, the practice may constitute further values that can only be instantiated or appreciated by engaging in that practice. I have to be more cautious here: I do not intend to claim that in order to understand what those values are, one must actually engage in the practice. My claim is that the relevant values are constituted by the practice. Once the practice is there, others can come to appreciate its values, at least to some extent, without actually taking part in it.[14]

It is worth noting that this kind of complexity is typically not present in the case of coordination conventions. When the reason for having a social rule consists in solving an antecedent (recurrent) coordination problem, then following the rule to solve the problem is more or less all that there is to it. (Notice that you can pretend to play chess; you cannot pretend to drive on the right side of the road, or pretend to spell a word correctly.)

If constitutive conventions tend to be responsive to a variety of human needs and values, as I claim that they do, you may wonder what makes such rules conventional at all. Basically, the answer consists in a combination of two facts: First, it is crucial to realize that the needs, functions, or values that such conventions respond to, radically *underdetermine* the content of the rules that constitute the relevant social practice. Our need or desire to play some competitive intellectual board game does not determine the content of the rules of chess; the creative needs or desires to stage dramatic performances do not determine the particular theatrical genres that have emerged over time in various cultures; the reasons for showing respect to people under various circumstances do not determine the particular practices of courtesy that various populations have.

Second, the reasons for following such constitutive rules are compliance-dependent reasons. The reasons for participating in a conventional practice crucially depend on the fact that the practice is there and its rules actually followed by the relevant population. Without some level of general compliance (in the

---

[14] This, of course, is a complicated and controversial issue; I have elaborated on some of the difficulties in my "Legal Positivism."

relevant population), there is no social practice. To the extent that anyone has a reason to participate, the reason partly depends on the fact that it is the practice that actually exists.

The combination of these two facts explains why constitutive rules of such practices are *arbitrary*, and thus conventional. In other the words, the conditions of conventionality outlined in the previous chapter clearly apply here. Looking at the game of chess, for example,[15] we can see that

1. there is a population that follows a set of rules, S_1, in circumstances C,
2. there are some reasons, call them A, for members of this population to follow S_1 in C, and
3. there are some alternative rules, S_2, that if members of that population had actually followed in circumstances C, then A would have been a sufficient reason for them to follow S_2 instead of S_1 in circumstances C, and at least partly because S_2 are the rules generally followed instead of S_1.

Basically, the idea is that chess could be played differently, and if it was played somewhat differently from they way it is—call this altered version chess*—it would have been a sufficient and compliance-dependent reason for potential players to follow those rules that are actually being followed by others, that is, to play chess* instead of chess. That is why the constitutive rules of chess are conventional.

An obvious objection can be raised here: one can claim that if the rules of chess, for instance, were different from what they are, it would not be chess, but some other game. The identity of the game is substantially determined by the rules that constitute it; and if the rules are significantly different, the game is different as well (viz., chess* is not chess).[16] I say "significantly"

---

[15] To be sure, I am not claiming that this is true of all games. I take the example of chess because it has become an elaborate social practice to play this game. Other games can simply be invented, and played by the invented rules, without becoming a conventional practice.

[16] It is not entirely clear that only the rules determine the identity of the practice. It is arguable that the identity of such a practice, like chess, is partly path dependent. Tim Williamson suggested to me that if we discover that Mar-

different because it is very doubtful that small changes in the rules allow us to say that it would be a different game. Suppose, for example, that we have two communities of chess players: one plays the game with a rule that allows castling, while the other community plays it without this rule. Would we say that these two populations play a different game? I doubt it. We should say that they both play chess, albeit somewhat differently. However, if we imagine differences that are more and more substantial, at some point we would have to say that it is no longer the same game (though it may still be quite similar in its main functions and values). Which is just another way of saying that such practices, like chess, are *constituted* by rules.

Now, it is true that the *identity* of a conventional practice crucially depends on its constitutive rules. But this does not mean that the rules cannot be conventional. As long as we can envisage alternatives to the rules that are actually being followed, that is, without any significant loss in the purpose or function of those rules, and the reasons for following the rules are compliance dependent, the rules are arbitrary and thus conventional in the requisite sense. It should not be difficult to imagine a board game that is very similar to chess, and instantiates basically the same points or values that chess does, but with rules that are somewhat different from the rules of chess. (Perhaps instead of sixty-four squares, we could have a board of eighty-one squares; or we could have different pieces, say two queens instead of one, etc.) In other words, we have to admit that there might be some difficult questions about what counts as an alternative way of doing, roughly, the same thing. But rough identity is all we need here. As long as we can envisage alternative rules that would basically achieve the same purpose(s) for the relevant population, or serve basically

tians play a game that is identical to chess (all the rules are the same, etc.), it is still not chess. My own view is that we do not have a clear intuition about this, and I suspect that the question of whether "Martian chess" is chess or not, is not answerable. Recall, however, that I have not assumed here that a social practice is identical with its constitutive rules. Thus, the mere fact that Martians have a game with identical rules does not necessarily entail that their game is identical to chess. There is more to a game than the rules that constitute it.

the same function(s), and so forth, we should have no problem
characterizing the rules as conventional.

There is, however, a certain caveat that needs to be mentioned.
Changes in different rules might have very different results.
Consider, for example, the game of tennis. Until quite recently,
it used to have a fairly strict dress code for the players. At some
point this dress code was largely discarded. Still, we would not
think that the game of tennis has changed. On the other hand, if
we change the rule about, say, the size of the ball, or the height
of the net, tennis might become a very different game. What
explains the fact that changes in certain rules might make it the
case that it is no longer the same practice, while changes in other
rules would not make much of a difference? What makes certain
rules or conventions more central to the nature of the practice
than others? I think that the answer to this must reside in the
kind of values that the constitutive rules give rise to. Some of the
values we associate with the activity of following the constitutive
rules are such that they are more *essential* to the kind of practice
that it is. The players' outfit is not essential to tennis, we think,
since it is not particularly relevant to the kind of things we value
or appreciate in the game. The particular kind of technical skills
that tennis players have to exhibit, on the other hand, is essential
to what tennis is. Hence changes in the rules that affect those
skills might amount to a change in the game itself.[17]

CONVENTIONAL SOCIAL PRACTICES

All this is still very sketchy, and more needs to be said about what
social practices are and how they are constituted by conventions.
I hope that the following general observations prove useful.

[17] Strangely enough, this kind of question has actually reached the U.S. Supreme Court in the case of *PGA v. Martin*, 532 U.S. 661. The question before the
court was whether the Americans with Disabilities Act requires the Professional
Golf Association to wave its rule of requiring all tournament competitors to walk
to the course. The majority of the court decided affirmatively, arguing that the
rule change would not affect the essential or fundamental character of the game.

The Systematic Nature of Conventional Practices

Constitutive conventions come in *systems* of rules.[18] This is an aspect of the typical, almost necessary, complexity of social practices. There is basically no such thing as a single-rule social practice. One might think that the example of a greeting convention is just such an instance. But I doubt that this is the case. Viewed as a social practice of "greetings"—assuming that it is legitimate to view it that way—even this simple case is probably more complex. In addition to the rule that requires greeting acquaintances in some conventional manner under certain circumstances, there must be some rules that determine what those circumstances are, who counts as an acquaintance for the purposes of this rule, how to deal with various exceptions (e.g., do you have to greet someone again if you had just greeted him a couple of hours ago?), and so on. To be sure, I am not suggesting that all these issues are necessarily covered by the conventions that prevail in the relevant community. Some of these issues would be, and others might remain unsettled by the existing conventions. Typically, however, social practices are complex, and the conventions that constitute social practices normally come in systems of rules.[19] Note that coordination conventions do not have this feature. A coordination convention can be fairly isolated, standing on its own, as it were, without forming part of an interlocking system of norms. The convention of saying "Hello" when picking up the phone, for example, solves a particular coordination problem that is not related to any particular social practice; it doesn't form part of a system of norms.

---

[18] The systematic nature of constitutive rules was emphasized by Searle, *Speech Acts*, 35–37. See also Raz on interlocking norms in his *Practical Reason and Norms*, 111–13.

[19] There is, of course, a question here about the individuation of norms/rules: it is not always easy to tell whether we face a single rule that is complex, or a conjunction of a number of rules. I take it, however, that a complete norm typically consists of the following components: a definition of the norm subjects, a designation of a certain norm-act or act type, a deontic operator (such as a duty, permission, right, etc.), and some circumstances that determine the application of the norm (which may, or may not, be implicitly determined by the characterization of the norm-act).

Division of Labor

It is typical of constitutive conventions that we tend to have a very partial knowledge of them. Most of us, for example, are aware that there are conventions constituting distinct genres of theater, and we can articulate some of them, but our knowledge is typically rather partial. We know, however, that others know what those conventions are. There are, in this field, as in many others, experts, or perhaps better, practitioners. But the dividing line between the practitioners, whose practice determines the conventions, and others, who are more or less aware of them, is not a sharp one. To the question "Whose convention is it?" there is rarely a simple answer. What we would normally see is a kind of division of labor: a core of practitioners, whose practices and self-understandings determine, to the greatest extent, what the conventions are, and additional groups of people in outer circles, whose knowledge of the conventions is much more partial, and whose influence on their content is relatively marginal. But again, the distinction between the relevant populations is not a hard and fast one; a complex division of labor may obtain, whereby even those groups who are relatively farther removed from the inner circle do affect, albeit in limited ways, the shape and content of the relevant conventions.

Perhaps a clear example of this can be given from the domain of law. Most people are only vaguely aware of the conventions that determine the sources of law of their country, and mostly, they rely on their lawyers to know what those conventions really are. Even within the legal circles, however, some groups are more important than others. Judges, and perhaps to a similar extent, legislators, play the crucial role. The conventions that determine what counts as law in the relevant legal system, are, first and foremost, the conventions of judges, particularly in the higher courts.[20] But in fact, other legal officials can also play various roles in determining the content of such conventions. The practices of administrative agencies, police officers, accountants, city councilors, and so on, all contribute some-

---

[20] For a discussion of these conventions see chapter 7.

thing to what the conventional practices are. So once again, the image I suggest is one of a division of labor, taking place in concentric circles; the closer one is to the center, the greater effect one has on what the convention is; and vice versa, of course. Generally speaking, however, most of us are, most of the time, in the outer circles, and we rely on others who know better; namely, on those whose practice it is.

Note that (almost) none of this is expected to obtain in the case of coordination conventions. Coordination conventions are there to solve a particular recurrent coordination problem. Such conventions cannot be expected to solve the coordination problem if most people are largely ignorant about their content. To be sure, I am not trying to suggest that people must be aware of the precise nature of the coordination problem that gave rise to the emergence of the convention. But they must be aware of the solution; otherwise the convention cannot fulfill its function as such a solution. Consider, for example, rules of spelling. Presumably, the rules of spelling are basically coordination conventions. Now, it is true that not everybody knows all the rules and not everybody spells words correctly. Some division of labor might apply here as well. But it would be very limited. Experts, though they may well exist, have very limited role in shaping the content of spelling conventions. Their role is typically limited to providing information about what the rules are (such as in dictionaries or textbooks). Once a word becomes misspelled by most of the relevant population, the misspelling becomes the standard one; it is no longer *mis*spelling if it is the actual spelling used by of most of the population. In other words, the role of experts or a core circle of practitioners is very limited in such cases.

The Interpretative Aspect of Constitutive Conventions

Constitutive conventions are typically prone to change over time. In this they do not necessarily differ from coordination conventions. The difference resides in the process of change, or more precisely, in the reasons for change. Coordination conventions serve specific functions in a specific set of circumstances (which may, or may not, include the agents' subjective

preferences). Coordination conventions are normative solutions
to some type of coordination problem. If the relevant normative solution that has evolved forms a stable equilibrium, then
as long as the circumstances remain constant, there would not
be any particular pressure for change. If the convention does
not constitute a stable equilibrium, a pressure may build up to
reach that stage, if circumstances allow. Sometimes, however,
the cost of change is higher than its potential gains, and therefore, even if there is a reason to shift to a better convention,
that reason may be defeated by the costs that are involved in the
change itself.[21] Now, all these considerations would normally
apply to constitutive conventions as well. However, in the latter
case, there is an additional factor that often affects the dynamics of change. Conventions constituting social practices constitute a whole grammar of, *inter alia*, evaluative concerns that
might come to affect the point, and consequently the content
and shape, of the constitutive conventions themselves. In other
words, constitutive conventions tend to be in a constant process
of interpretation and reinterpretation that is partly affected by
external values, but partly by those same values that are constituted by the conventional practice itself. The rapid changes that
occurred in the conventions of the visual arts in the early part of
the twentieth century provide a dramatic example of this process. Some of the pressure for change came from external influ-
ences of a rapidly changing world, such as mass industrialization
and dramatic political events. However, some of the pressure
for change came from novel interpretations of those old values
that were thought to be constitutive of the genre. Artists have
gradually realized, for instance, that the point of a painting need
not be achieved by a figurative composition; once this dramatic
shift occurred, in the form of Cubist and mainly abstract paintings, the constitutive conventions of painting also underwent

---

[21] For example, think about the remarkable durability of spelling conventions. Some of them are rather cumbersome and their rationale path-dependent,
but it often takes centuries for spelling conventions to change. Presumably, at
least part of the explanation for this might be that the cost of change is too high
relative to the expected gain.

a considerable change. Thus, just as the constitutive conventions establish some of the values associated with the practice, changes in the prevailing interpretations of those values tend to change the conventions that initially constituted them. We may safely assume that the more a given practice tends to be interpretative, and the values associated with it potentially contentious, the more likely it is that such changes will occur.

History and Path Dependency

So far, we have noted that a social practice constituted by conventions is systematic, involving different kinds of constitutive rules, allowing for a complex division of labor between different kinds of practitioners, and that the constitutive conventions tend to be under interpretative pressure that may account for ways in which such conventions change over time. What is still missing here, however, is the history of the practice and its significance. Constitutive conventions tend to develop over a long period of time. Unlike institutional rules, they are not enacted; they develop gradually and their content is path dependent. In other words, constitutive conventions have a history, and the history tends to be socially significant. An understanding of the history of a conventional practice typically contributes to a better understanding of the nature of the practice, its inherent values, and its significance for the population that practices it. Needless to say, this historic significance may vary between different types of practices; for some practices history is more significant than for others. For example, the historical dimension of games, like chess, is relatively insignificant; it only preoccupies those who have a special interest in it. But for most genres of art, to take a conspicuous example, history is crucial. For instance, one cannot understand the nature of contemporary avant-garde theater without knowing what previous genres and conventions of theater it rebels against. It is often part of the point of such conventions that they rebel against (or otherwise seek to modify) previous conventions.

Now, you may think that this is an aspect of the nature of art, not of the nature of conventional practices generally. To some extent this is true, but not entirely. Many other conventional practices have this feature, namely, that some of their constitutive conventions evolve as a response to, or modification of, previous conventions. For example, conventions of fashion tend to have this feature, as do some norms of courtesy or etiquette and, generally, conventional practices that tend to be particularly responsive to social trends and developments. In general, this is one aspect of the dynamic nature of constitutive conventions. Since they tend to constitute some of the values inherent in the relevant practice, those values would normally call for interpretation and reevaluation over time, and this process is likely to bring changes in the constitutive conventions themselves.

Codification and Institutional Practices

Rules that emerge as social conventions often get to be institutionally codified at some point. This is true of both coordination and constitutive conventions. Now one may wonder whether codified conventions are still conventions. Basically, the answer depends on the kind of codification that occurs. There are two ways in which conventions can be codified: I will call them *legislative codification* and *encyclopedic codification*.

Legislative codification of rules purports to determine, authoritatively, what the rules are. If legislative codification of conventions succeeds, the practice is no longer conventional. It becomes an institutional practice. In contrast, encyclopedic codification only purports to report what the rules are, without actually determining their content for the future. Thus, regardless of how successful encyclopedic codification is, such codification leaves the conventional nature of the practice in its place. Chess, for example, was codified in the early twentieth century in Europe.[22] The codification of the rules of chess is probably a legislative codification. The rules followed in chess tournaments are those that have been codified by the relevant

---

[22] As far as I could ascertain, the first official international codification of chess rules occurred in 1929, by FIDE, the World Chess Federation, in Venice.

institutions. (You may wonder, then, why have I used the example of chess as a conventional practice if it is no longer conventional, at least since 1929. The answer is that I think that chess is still a conventional game when played by amateurs who care little about official tournaments, and just play the game, roughly, as conventions determine it. I suspect that this is now true about most sports; they are practiced in two spheres, as it were—an official, institutional sphere, that regulates official leagues and tournaments, and an unofficial, amateur, noninstitutional sphere, by and large still conventional.)

Dictionaries and grammar textbooks provide a prominent example of encyclopedic codification of social conventions. Dictionaries do not purport to determine, authoritatively, what the rules for using words are, but only to report common usage as determined by the social conventions. Those aspects of language use that are conventional remain so, even when the conventions are codified in dictionaries and textbooks. If a change occurs in the relevant conventions, the dictionaries and textbooks need to be revised, not the other way around. Roughly, then, legislative codification determines and modifies the content of the rules, whereas encyclopedic codification only indicates what the rules are. Thus, we are entitled to say that legislative codification of social conventions typically replaces the conventions by institutional rules, whereas encyclopedic codification leaves the conventional aspect of the rules in its place. Admittedly, this is somewhat rough, because some exceptions are possible. For instance, legislative codification may fail, to some extent, and then it may become partly encyclopedic even if it purported to legislate. And vice versa, it may happen that a long-standing encyclopedic codification actually amounts to a kind of legislative code that determines the content of the relevant rules. Nevertheless, I think that the distinction is pretty clear and mostly unproblematic.

The institutionalization that results from legislative codification of social practices tends to bring with it two main modifications: first, it creates a mechanism for change. As H.L.A. Hart has observed, institutional practices typically have a set of *secondary rules*, that is, they have rules about their rules, such as rules determining ways in which new rules can be enacted and old ones modified.[23] Conventional practices typically lack such mechanisms. Conventions, as we have noted, are not enacted, they evolve gradually over time. Second, institutionalization typically involves the introduction of a mechanism for ensuring compliance with the rules. Institutional practices typically have rules that determine sanctions for violation of its rules, and a whole mechanism that determines how to monitor noncompliance, how to administer the sanctions, who gets to determine such matters, and so forth. Once again, conventional practices typically lack sanction mechanisms. Sanctions for noncompliance of conventional rules tend to be informal, mostly consisting in social pressure and hostile reaction of others in the population. Note that there is a connection between these two mechanisms: precisely because conventional practices lack a mechanism for administering sanctions, the conventions can change over time as a result of successive deviations from the rules. If a certain deviation is widespread and consistent enough, it is likely to engender a new rule, modifying or substituting the old one.

CONVENTIONS AND COOPERATION

Let me conclude this chapter by responding to some possible objections and adding a few clarifications. In particular, I want to consider the possible objection that the account of conventional practices I have given here ignores the essential cooperative nature of social practices. The claim does not have to be that all conventions are necessarily coordinative, but that in some sense, all social practices are. We cannot have a social practice, the objection is, unless it is the case that participants in the practice aim for some social coordination or cooperation, at least at some

---

[23] See *The Concept of Law*, chap. 5. The relevant distinction Hart introduced is between primary rules, namely, those that purport to guide conduct, and secondary rules that are rules about rules, not (directly) about conduct. Hart was mostly interested in the law, but his point about secondary rules can be easily generalized.

general level. According to this view, then, social practices are necessarily cooperative ventures; without such an underlying intention to cooperate, practices cannot be rendered intelligible. With two caveats that I will mention shortly, I see no particular difficulty with this suggestion. In fact, it may well be the case that some underlying cooperative aim, general and abstract as it may be, is part of the rationale of the compliance-dependent reasons for following the constitutive rules of a social practice. In other words, it seems to me plausible to assume that conventional practices tend to persist only if there is some background intention, or at least willingness, to cooperate that (most) participants in the practice share. I doubt that this is a necessary condition, and I think that it is even more doubtful that every participant in a conventional practice must actually entertain some underlying cooperative intention. The important point, however, is to keep these two issues separate: the main function of constitutive conventions is to constitute a social practice and regulate conduct within the practice. As I have argued at length, there is no need to assume that the main rationale of such conventions is to solve an antecedent recurrent coordination problem. This is quite compatible with the view, under discussion here, that it is a condition of the existence of social practices, or at least of their ability to be sustained and flourish, that a certain cooperative aim or intention is shared by most of its participants.[24]

Before we proceed to the caveats I mentioned, let me distinguish this idea about cooperative aims from a seemingly similar view, espoused by Searle, maintaining that social facts, generally speaking, require a certain form of *collective intentionality* in order to become facts of a social kind. Searle's thesis about the necessity of collective intentionality is a metaphysical one; he sees it as a necessary building block of the bridge leading

---

[24] An elaborate account of joint actions and their corresponding cooperative intentions is suggested by Michael Bratman in his work on shared agency (see "Shared Agency," in his *Faces of Intention*). Whether Bratman's account can be extended to cover large-scale cooperative ventures is a difficult question I need not try to consider here. (Scott Shapiro is currently working on this in the context of legal philosophy.) For a different, nonreductionist approach, see Tuomela, *The Philosophy of Sociality*.

from brute facts to social facts, by allowing the assignment of function to facts of the brute kind, thus assigning a new, social status to those kind of facts.[25] Now this is not the kind of view that I intend to discuss here. My discussion of constitutive conventions is not meant to say anything about the metaphysics of social reality, or about the ways in which brute facts are distinguishable from social facts (to the extent that the distinction itself is sensible, which I tend to doubt). In other words, whether Searle is right or wrong about the essential role of collective intentionality in explicating the concept of a social fact is an issue I do not need to grapple with.[26]

So now the caveats: first, we must make room for the possibility that the general cooperative aim(s) of the social practice is such that it allows for different and competing conceptions of this aim(s), along the lines suggested by Gallie in his discussion of "essentially contested concepts." According to Gallie, there are five conditions for a concept to be essentially contested: (1) The concept must be "apprasive," in that it stands for some kind of valued achievement. (2) This achievement must be internally complex, and (3) any explanation of its worth must refer to the respective contributions of its various parts or features. (4) The accredited achievement must be of a kind that admits of modifications in light of changing circumstances. And, finally, (5) each party recognizes the fact that its own understanding of the concept is contested by other parties.[27]

Admittedly, not all social practices would have these features. Their organizing aims and concepts may not be of this "apprasive" (or sufficiently complex) kind. But many social practices do conform to Gallie's description. Therefore, we must recognize that social practices can exist and flourish, even if the participants in the practice have competing and incompatible conceptions of the main reasons for participating in it, or

---

[25] See his *Construction of Social Reality*, 23–26, 37–39, 46.

[26] Later, in chapter 5, I will have something to say against Searle's theory about the relations between constitutive rules and speech acts of the performative kind, doubting that those relations are as essential as Searle maintains; but that, again, is not a metaphysical issue.

[27] See Gallie, "Essentially Contested Concepts," 171–80.

competing conceptions of the values the practice instantiates. The only assumption we have to make here is that in the case of conventional practices, the reasons for following the rules are compliance dependent. But this does pose any particular problems in this context. X's reasons for following R might be such that they partly depend on Y's and Z's compliance with R (and assume that Y's reasons depend on X's and Z's compliance, etc.), even if the reasons X, Y, and Z have for following R are different and incompatible. Perhaps there is a practical limit to how much incompatible such reasons can be, that is, for a practice to be socially sustainable, but that is basically an empirical matter that is likely to vary from case to case.

The second caveat is this: we should not assume that participation in a conventional social practice is necessarily voluntary. In this respect, many conventional practices are not like chess, which you can easily decide to play or not to play. Roughly, there are two kinds of social practices in this respect: those that potential participants need to opt in to, and those in which we are participants by default, as it were, and the only relevant question is whether we can opt out of them. Let us call them voluntary and involuntary practices, respectively. Examples of voluntary practices include such practices as playing games and artistic endeavors. Examples of involuntary practices would be those that form part of our everyday social interactions, like speaking a language and following norms of etiquette or courtesy. Now the point is that opting out of an involuntary conventional practice might be very costly, socially or otherwise. Consider, for example, practices of etiquette, like a greeting convention, or table manners. If you decide not to play the game, so to speak, you are very likely to face some hostile reaction and social sanctions. People will think the worse of you for not playing the game, and you might find yourself socially condemned or isolated. Perhaps you are willing the pay the price, but a high price it might be.[28] Similar considerations apply to

---

[28] Needless to say, this is not a moral judgment; in some cases opting out might be the right thing to do. Some of the moral significance of this feature of conventional practices I discuss in chapter 6.

the conventional aspects of language use. Some level of "opting out" is possible, in fact quite familiar from poor, substandard, uses of language. But typically such substandard uses are subject to social criticism and are often met with hostile reaction. And, needless to say, beyond a certain level, opting out is almost impossible, as it entails an inability to use language. To conclude this point: even if we admit that some cooperative intentions or attitudes must be largely present for a social practice to exist, we should be careful not to exaggerate this point and, in particular, we should not be tempted to assume that it entails voluntary participation.

A final clarification: it was not my intention in these remarks about conventional practices to monopolize the use of the words "social practice." Many practices can be called by that name, and they may not fit the account I gave here. For example, there is a custom in our department to have a drinks party every Friday afternoon with our graduate students. There is nothing wrong in calling this a social practice. I doubt, however, that it is a conventional practice in the sense we have defined here. Many customs or practices are created and sustained by agreement between the relevant parties, and I think that this Friday drinks party is such a case. Some practices that are brought to life by agreement between the relevant agents may turn into conventional practices after a while, but this is certainly not necessary. Be this as it may, my purpose here was to identify a certain type of social conventions and ways in which they constitute social practices. Other uses of the term "social practice" are certainly possible, and there is nothing in my remarks that would suggest otherwise.

You may still worry that constitutive conventions are doing too much work here. On the one had, they are responsive to a variety of needs and values that give rise to their emergence (besides coordination, that is). On the other hand, the conventions also constitute elaborate practices and give rise to values and modes of appreciation that, I claim, could not have otherwise emerged. There is a suspicion that perhaps too much weight is put here on conventional rules, as opposed to other aspects of social practices that are not directly related to their conventional nature. I believe that an answer to this concern will emerge after we see that conventions are not only at the surface of social activities. We need the idea that there are deep conventions, and this will be the topic of the next chapter.

Chapter Three

Deep Conventions

The Idea of Deep Conventions

In many cases it is quite clear that a normative practice is conventional. Nobody doubts that greetings are conventions; or that the notational rules of language that determine the sound-sense relations are conventional. In other cases, however, the conventionality of the relevant domain is genuinely controversial. To mention a few of examples that will be discussed later, the conventionality of performative speech acts is controversial; or, in the moral domain, the conventionality of norms of promising is controversial; as we shall seen in chapter 7, the conventional foundations of law are highly controversial. And there are many other such examples. There is something puzzling about such controversies. If conventions are only at the surface of human activities, regulating ways of doing this or that, it should be quite perspicuous whether a certain set of norms is conventional or not. The fact that the conventionality of various domains is not always transparent would seem to suggest that conventions can operate at deeper levels. I think that this is correct, and I will argue that for many surface conventions to be possible at all, a deeper set of conventions must be present. In this chapter I will try to show that deep conventions differ from surface conventions in the following ways:

  1. Deep conventions emerge as normative responses to basic social and psychological needs. They serve relatively basic functions in our social world.

2. Deep conventions typically enable a set of surface conventions to emerge, and many types of surface conventions are only made possible as instantiations of deep conventions.

3. Under normal circumstances, deep conventions are actually practiced by following their corresponding surface conventions.

4. Compared with surface conventions, deep conventions are typically much more durable and less amenable to change.

5. Surface conventions often get to be codified and thus replaced by institutional rules. Deep conventions typically resist codification (of this kind).

Needless to say, all this is very schematic and needs to be shown. The argument is presented as follows: I begin with an outline of what deep conventions are, using examples from language, competitive games, and art. This initial account is followed by a detailed reply to three possible objections to the idea that there are deep conventions. I conclude with an account of some further differences between deep and surface conventions, and a few thoughts on the importance of the distinction.

Games

I would like to begin with a few examples from different social domains. Consider, first, the rules constituting the game of chess. As we have seen in detail, the rules constituting chess are constitutive conventions. They constitute what chess is and how to play the game. In part, they constitute the point of playing the game and some of the specific values associated with it. But all this is possible only against the background of a deeper layer of some shared normative scheme about what competitive games are. Such normative backgrounds are what I call deep conventions. Chess, as a game of a particular kind, is only an instantiation of a more general, norm-governed, human activity that we call "playing a (competitive) game."

Admittedly, it is not easy to define a particular set of norms that constitute the activity we would call "playing a competitive game." Nevertheless, some underlying conventions are clear enough:

(1). Playing a competitive game is basically a rule-constituted activity. This means at least three main things. First, that in
playing a game, the participants follow some rules; following
certain rules is part of what playing a game is. Second, that
the rules of the game define, among other things, what the
game is, what counts as success or failure in the game, what
kind of skills or achievements the game values, and so on.
Third, the rules of games purposefully create certain chal-
lenges that basically determine the kinds of skills that participants have to exhibit in playing the game. In other words, it
is typical of games that their rules are there to make things
somehow more difficult, rather than easy, in getting from A
to B, so to speak.[1] Now, of course, these norms can be violated, so that putative players might break the rules or deviate from them in various ways.

(2). Games involve a certain element of detachment from real-
life concerns. The level of detachment varies considerably
between different types of games, and in different contexts
and cultures. But even when the detachment from real-life
concerns is minimal, games have a certain artificiality that
is quite essential to our understanding of what games are. A
violation of such norms typically involves a confusion; it often manifests a misunderstanding of what games are or what
the situation is.

(3). Games have a fairly sharp demarcation of participants. Players are typically recognized as such and can be distinguished
quite clearly from spectators, fans, and other nonparticipants.
Again, these are norms that can be violated on particular occasions, for example, when fans or spectators attempt to participate as players and thus disrupt the game.

Let me clarify two points here. First, these three features are
meant to be examples of deep conventions determining what
games in our culture are. This list is not meant to be exhaustive, of course, and it is certainly not meant to be a definition of

---

[1] This last point was nicely noted by Thomas Hurka in his *Perfectionism*,
123–28.

what (competitive) games are.[2] Second, I do not wish to claim that first we must have an abstract concept of games, and then we can invent concrete instances of the abstract concept. This is not how our social and conceptual world develops. Abstract concepts emerge gradually, I presume, concomitantly with the particular cases that they instantiate. In order to play a game like chess, I argue, participants (players and spectators) must also share a normative background about what playing a game is. I have yet to prove, of course, that such background norms are conventions. For now, the point is that without such a background normative scheme of what, say, a competitive game is, the specific conventions constituting particular games, like chess, would not make sense; they would not be possible at all.

Art

Perhaps the best example of a deep convention would be one that has clearly changed over time. Consider, for example, the conventions of visual arts in medieval Europe since early Middle Ages until, roughly, the end of the fifteenth century. One of its underlying themes consisted in a perception of the visual arts as a religious tool of glorifying God and vividly telling the story of the Bible. In Christian Europe, this religious function was instantiated by a convention that paintings and sculptures were supposed to represent a certain image of the world, mostly the legendary world of the Bible. In sharp contrast, however, the basic convention of Islamic art, roughly at the same time, was ornamental (and textual), nonrepresentational. That is, in spite of the very similar underlying religious function of Islamic art, to glorify God and tell the story of the Koran. In other words, the representational form of Christian art and the ornamental form of Islamic art, though both motivated by very similar social-religious concerns, engendered very different

[2] At this point I do not need to take a stance on the question of whether "game" is a family resemblance concept, as Wittgenstein has famously maintained. In the next chapter I will raise some doubts about Wittgenstein's account of family resemblance concepts.

genres of visual arts, each based on its own deep conventions, one basically representational and the other almost exclusively ornamental.

Language

Finally, consider some taxonomical conventions of a natural language. Most simple nouns, for instance, "desk," "book," or "vegetable," function, basically, as labels of sets. Such words are names of categories of objects. Now, the sound-sense relations (and, generally, notation) are conventional. As we shall see in the next chapter, such conventions are paradigmatic examples of Lewis-type coordination conventions. It is a surface convention of the English language that desks (the objects) are called "desk." However, we can only name such a category of objects by a certain word if we possess their concept as a distinct category. And the point is that we can often imagine a language that categorizes such objects differently than we do. Admittedly, natural kinds are different: it is more likely that we encounter instances of a natural phenomenon or set of things, and then we just assume that they have some properties in common that would make us use a word for them all, whatever those properties really are, or turn out to be. In this case, naming does not presuppose a grasp of the concept of the relevant category, at least not an elaborate one. In the case of nonnatural kinds, however, the categorizations we employ in language are often quite conventional. The distinction between natural and nonnatural, conventional categorizations, however, is often rather difficult to determine.

Consider this passage from Borges, cited by Foucault: "This passage quotes 'a certain Chinese Encyclopedia' in which it is written that 'animals' are divided into (a) belonging to the Emperor, (b) embalmed, (c) tame, (d) sucking pigs, (e) sirens, (f) fabulous, (g) stray dogs, (h) included in the present classification, (i) frenzied, (j) innumerable, (k) drawn with a very fine camelhair brush, (l) *et cetera*."[3] And then Foucault rightly notes

---

3 In the preface of his *The Order of Things*.

that "the wonderment of this taxonomy . . . is demonstrated as the exotic charm of another system of thought . . . the stark impossibility of thinking *that*."[4] Even if it is not literally impossible to think *that* of "kinds of animals," surely it is very remote from what we think. The world in which this "certain Chinese Encyclopedia" has been written, and let us assume here that there is such a world, must have been very different from ours. But this is just a reflection of the fact that we have our own world of taxonomical concepts and categories, a world in which "sirens" and "drawn with a very fine camelhair brush" are not associated with "kinds of animals."[5]

I take it that none of this is philosophical news.[6] What remains to be seen is whether any of this complex background that enables the formation of surface conventions is itself conventional in a meaningful sense. Before we proceed, however, a clarification is called for: What does it mean to say that one set of conventions "enables" the emergence of another? Basically, it means that (1) without the existence of deep conventions the relevant surface conventions would not be possible, that such norms could not have emerged without being instances of the deep conventions; and that (2) in following surface conventions one also follows, albeit indirectly, the deep conventions that underlie it. In other words, surface conventions instantiate

---

4 Ibid.

5 Perhaps this may look similar to "grue" from Goodman's "new riddle of induction" (see his *Fact, Fiction, and Forecast*). But my point here is quite the opposite. The question for Goodman is why "grue" would not work, even if it is logically or epistemically just as warranted as "green." In Foucault's example, I assume the contrary; I assume that sometimes these weird categories, that make no sense in our language, *do work* in some other language. If Foucault's example turns out to be something like "grue" (viz., nonprojectible), the example is not good. Other examples however, could easily be found, and I discuss some more mundane translation issues further in the sequel. For some of the main literature on the "grue" problem, see Stalker, *Grue*.

6 See, for example, Wittgenstein's famous discussion of "form of life" as a precondition of language use, in his *Philosophical Investigations*, §142, 241–42. See also Searle, "Literal Meaning," and *The Construction of Social Reality*, 127–47, though Searle clearly assumes that understanding of literal meaning depends on underlying shared beliefs and intentions, not norms.

deep conventions. Note that in saying that P *instantiates* Q, we do not suggest that Q causes P. This is not a causal relation. (As an analogy, consider the relations between certain aspects of language and thought; that certain thoughts depend on having language competency, are enabled by it, does not entail that linguistic concepts cause the thoughts that employ them. A thought, some mental content, as it were, may instantiate one's mastery of language, but not caused by it.)

Let us return to the example of the representational convention of visual arts. In order to show that such norms are conventions, we need to show that they satisfy the conditions of conventionality outlined in chapter 1. Thus, first we must show that there is a community that follows the norms when creating works of art of a certain kind. This, I take it, is an observable fact. Then, it must be the case that there were certain reasons to follow the representational convention, reasons that explain the nature of visual arts at the time and the values associated with it. I will assume here that this is not a problem, and that we could articulate the reasons for the representational aspect of art at the time. Finally, we need to show that such norms constituting the nature of visual arts were arbitrary in the requisite sense. But were they?

For a norm, R, to be a convention it must be the case that there is an alternative norm, S, that members of the relevant population could have followed instead, achieving, basically, the same purpose. Now, the availability of S, in this case, is not a concern: we know that there are nonrepresentational ways of creating works of visual art. In fact we know more, we know that there are nonrepresentational ways of creating art of a very similar kind, namely, basically religious. But there is a concern here about the question of alternatives: Suppose we compare the representational norm of visual arts in medieval Europe with the nonrepresentational, ornamental, norm of Islamic art at the time. Would it be right to assume that these two cultures have had different conventions that constitute different ways of doing, roughly, the same thing? Perhaps not; it is sometimes difficult to determine an answer to such questions, partly because the criteria of sameness here are vague. We have already encountered this problem in the previous chapter. The identify of conventional practices is crucially determined by their constitutive rules. Hence it is often problematic to determine what counts as an alternative way of doing roughly the same thing. But as we noted there, rough identity is all we need here. As long as we can envisage alternative rules that would basically achieve the same purposes or serve the same functions for the relevant population, we should have no problem characterizing the relevant norms as conventional. Similarly, in the case of deep conventions that constitute forms of art, it is probably right to assume that small, gradual changes in the conventions still constitute the same kind of art, just in different ways. But, admittedly, at some point it might become very difficult to say that alternative norms constitute different ways of doing the same thing. Thus, perhaps we cannot have a determinate answer to the question of whether Islamic art and Christian art (say, from the eleventh through the fourteenth centuries) were just different ways of doing roughly the same thing, or not. But this does not necessarily pose a difficulty for realizing that both sets of normative frameworks for creating visual arts at the time were basically conventional. We know from later developments in each of these genres that those conventions have changed, and quite radically, in fact.

There is another complication here. Surface conventions often come in layers with different degrees of shallowness, so to speak. The deep conventions of representational art in medieval Europe, for instance, were instantiated by an elaborate set of surface conventions. But some of those surface conventions were probably deeper than others. I would guess that conventions of religious symbolism, composition, and perspective were deeper than specific conventions of, say, color symbolism (e.g., that blue represents virginity); and conventions of color symbolism may have been deeper than conventions about paint material or the size of the works, and so on. Similar degrees of shallowness are present in other cases. The deep conventions of theater, to take another example, are instantiated by surface conventions of particular genres of theater, and those, in turn, may be practiced by following even shallower conventions, say, about the number of acts, stage setting, and so forth.

If this is the case, you may wonder whether there is a categorical distinction between deep and surface conventions at all; perhaps we are only entitled to say that there are differences of degree, that some conventions are deeper than others. In response, two points: First, it should be noted that deep conventions can rarely be followed on their own, as it were; deep conventions are actually practiced by following their corresponding surface conventions. When we play competitive games we follow the deep conventions that constitute what competitive games are by following the surface conventions of particular games. Surface conventions, on the other hand, can be followed on their own even if there are further, even shallower conventions, that people follow in those circumstances as well.

Another main difference between the deep and the surface conventions is that the deep is constitutive of the practice in ways that the idea of *deeper than* does not capture. Without the deep conventions of theater (such as, for example, the convention about suspension of belief), there is no theater, at least not in any form that we are familiar with. Without the deep conventions of competitive games that we mentioned above, there would not be a practice that we can call "competitive games." The deep conventions constitute what the practice is. In contrast, the surface conventions that are deeper than others do not necessarily serve this constitutive function (though sometimes they may). For example, a convention about color symbolism could easily be replaced with a different one (say, a different color or none at all), without any necessary relation to the deeper conventions about the religious significance of the work, composition, perspective, and so on. Surface conventions generally *instantiate* the deeper ones; they are different ways of *doing that*. Shallower conventions within the setting of other surface conventions do not necessarily instantiate the deeper ones. Their relation to the deeper conventions is typically more incidental.

Note, however, that even if I am wrong about this, and the most we can say is that conventions come in layers, some deeper than others, my basic contention that there are deep conventions remains basically intact. Even if there are just layers of depths and shallowness, it can still be the case, as I argue here, that many shallow conventions instantiate deeper ones; and that without the relevant deeper layer, certain shallow conventions could not have emerged.

Examples cannot settle the question of whether the norms that enable the formation of surface conventions are conventions. There are probably three main reasons to doubt that they are. First, it might be argued that the kind of background norms I have in mind here are widely shared beliefs, not norms, and beliefs (as we saw in chapter 1) are not the kind of things that can be conventions. Second, it can be argued that even if they are norms, such norms are not conventions because they are not arbitrary in the requisite sense. Finally, it can be objected that deep conventions are just abstractions of reasons to follow conventions, and not social rules at all. The discussion in the following section aims to answer these concerns.

Norms, Beliefs, and Reasons

Social conventions are norms people follow. Conventions are not beliefs. It is a difficult question, but one we need not try to answer here, what the kind of beliefs are that one must have in order to *follow* a rule (as opposed to just acting in accordance with a rule). As we saw in chapter 1, following a rule does require a certain level of awareness on part of the agent that he is complying with a norm, which requires, in turn, a certain level of awareness that there is a norm that applies to the circumstances. On the other hand, it is quite clearly the case that people can follow norms that they cannot explicitly formulate, or formulate correctly. In any case, the rule, or the norm, is the convention, and not the agents' belief that there is a rule.

Generally, if N is a norm, then to know what N is, is to know *how* to go about doing something, or at least what it takes to do it, or such. Actually following a norm is typically a form of action, manifest in the way you do things. Now consider the example of the visual arts I have mentioned earlier. I claimed that the idea of representation was a deep convention of visual arts in a certain culture. The objection we are considering now consists in the claim that the representational aspect of art was basically a shared understanding about the nature of visual arts, that it was basically a belief, or a set of beliefs, not norms, and therefore not conventions either. But this is not the case. The convention that visual arts must purport to represent a visual biblical image has all the characteristics of a norm: artists were generally expected to follow the norm, they had to follow it by actions, typically manifesting certain abilities or skills, and deviations from the norm would have been met with criticism or hostility.

In this respect, creating a work of art is very much like playing a game. To know what games are, is mostly a know-how; it consists in an array of abilities to participate in a social practice that is essentially normative. Think about the ways in which young children learn to play competitive games: it is not something that they learn by theoretical instruction. Children learn how to play (competitive) games by playing them. It is mostly a social skill that they acquire, not a form of knowledge that such and such is the case. In learning how to play games (or how to create works of art of a certain kind, for that matter), children learn to follow rules and social norms.

Just in order to clarify: it is not part of my understanding of what following a norm consists in that *knowing how* is categorically different from *knowing that*. It may well be the case, as Stanley and Williamson argue,[7] that knowing how is a species of knowing that. In any case, it is a unique species and one that is probably not reducible to *knowledge that*.[8] Nor do I wish to claim that every type of knowing how necessarily involves abilities or skills. Surely there is a sense in which one knows how to do something without actually being able to perform it. (Generally speaking, I suspect that the concept of knowing how is inherently ambiguous between knowing how that involves abilities or skills, and knowing how that does not. If somebody asks me whether I know how to play chess, then the answer is both yes and no. Yes, I know how to play chess in the sense

---

[7] Stanley and Williamson, "Knowing How."
[8] As Stanley and Williamson explicitly admit (ibid., 433–34).

that I know the rules and I know what it takes to win. But no, I don't really know how to play chess since I have never actually played the game and I would certainly lose to any reasonable player in just a few moves. And this is crucially different from the distinction between knowing how to φ and knowing how to φ well. In any case, it is not part of my argument to substantiate this claim. I am content with the modest assumption that following a norm typically involves a form of knowing how.)

Perhaps you may doubt that this is also the case with the kind of knowledge that underlies conventions of language. We have to be cautious here. I do not intend to claim that our entire linguistic-conceptual world is determined by some deep conventions or, indeed, that all linguistic knowledge is a form of knowing how. Surely a great deal, perhaps most, of what makes our concepts and linguistic categories possible consists in beliefs we share about the world, our innate capacities, and, to some extent, by the way the world actually is.[9] I have no intention of denying this. But even so, it would be difficult to deny that a significant aspect of our language use and concept formation is governed by norms (not necessarily conventional, of course). In other words, it is plausible to maintain that numerous concepts and categories we use in a natural language manifest a *know how* that is, indeed, analogous to playing a game. If this is the case, then we have established their normative aspect. Playing a game is undoubtedly a norm governed behavior.

As an example, consider one of the main reasons for difficulties we encounter in translation. Some concepts and linguistic categories are determined by a complex know-how that takes time and a great deal of habituation to acquire. When you have acquired the mastery of using a concept in a certain language that is absent in another, you may find it very difficult to express the concept in the language of those who have not acquired that particular set of know-how. When you look at the list of "kinds of animals" in that "certain Chinese encyclopedia," and realize the "stark impossibility of thinking *that*," to use Foucault's expression, what you partly realize is that we lack the skills, the

[9] See, for example, Quine, "Natural Kinds."

extensive habituation, to even think about kinds of animals in that way. This is why it is indeed so difficult to imagine *that*, or to translate it to our language.[10]

I know that this Chinese dictionary is an extreme example (and knowing the source, one should suspect that it is imaginary). But less exotic examples are abundant in contemporary natural languages. For example, there is a word in Hebrew, pronounced "davka," that is simply impossible to translate to English (or to any other language that I know of). One would say, for example, "I will davka go to the party tonight." Very roughly, "davka" means here something like this: "in spite of some vague background expectation to the contrary." But even this is too rough (as, for example, "davka" may imply or insinuate something like "for spite," depending on the context), and the nuances of its use in Hebrew just cannot be conveyed in any straightforward translation. It takes some practice and habituation in Hebrew to use "davka" correctly. You just have to learn how to play the game.

The point here needs to be qualified, though. First, I do not wish to claim that all the differences between natural languages that are difficult to translate result from differences in deep conventions. Some translation difficulties might be due to differences in perceptual discriminations between different communities that allow one community to have certain concepts that other communities lack. The famous example of the Eskimos having numerous concepts of snow is a case in point (that is, if they really do; I have been told that this is just a myth). And there may be other explanations for difficulties in translation. Second, and more important, I certainly do not claim here that the *literal meaning* of most words we use in a natural language is conventionally determined. On the contrary, in the next chapter we will see that in most cases, the norms constituting literal meaning are not conventions. The kind of categories and conventional norms discussed here constitute the reference

---

[10] What I have in mind here may well be an instance of Goodman's notion of *entrenchment*. I am not sure. If it is such an example, it may show that some forms of entrenchment are a matter of convention.

of words and categories we use in a natural language, not the norms that constitute the literal meaning of words, as such.[11]

The normative aspect of what I call deep conventions does not prove that such norms are, indeed, conventions. You may still doubt that they are really conventional. Or perhaps you might concede that some of the more trivial examples are conventions, but then you would insist that they are still pretty much at the surface. It is easy to concede, I take it, that as English speakers we differentiate between objects that we call "desk" and those that we call "tables," and that this categorization is basically conventional. It is easy to imagine some alternative categorizations of such objects that would have served us just as well. But then you might resist the idea that we do not associate "belonging to the Emperor," "frenzied," and "drawn with a very fine camelhair brush," with *kinds of animals*, as something that is, ultimately, conventional. After all, we have elaborate scientific theories about what *kinds* of such things are, and therefore we know that these are not kinds of animals. The problem, then, is not that we cannot imagine alternatives to what kinds of animals there are, but that such alternatives would be false.

This objection is too quick, however. It assumes that the "certain Chinese Encyclopedia" basically purports to refer to "kinds" in roughly the same way that we do. In other words, it assumes that "kinds" in Chinese of this imaginary world really translates to "kinds" in contemporary English, and then the differences that remain can be expressed in terms of propositional content, whereby we are right and they were wrong.[12] This, of course, is a possibility, but it is not the only possibility.

[11] Needless to say, this requires some explanation and a careful distinction of literal meaning from other aspects of language use. I provide all this background in the next chapter.

[12] In other words, the objection assumes that "kinds of animals" in the Chinese dictionary was meant to be a "natural kind" predicate, and that the dictionary simply assumed a wrong theory about its reference. Or perhaps the objection can be worked out on the basis of a claim that "kinds of animals" can be carved out of the "natural joints of reality," objectively, as it were. See Hirsch, *Dividing Reality*, chap. 3 (though Hirsch raises important doubts about whether this works, even in simpler cases).

It is conceivable that such a straightforward translation is impossible here, as in so many other cases. Perhaps as impossible as it would be to translate the word "chess," or "game," into a language of speakers who have never played any games and have no such concept in their language. To be sure, I am not claiming that this is the case, I am just pointing out the possibility that it might be.

The point here is not confined to difficulties in translation. Other aspects of language exemplify the same point. Consider this legal case (from 1893) that reached the Supreme Court, *Nix v. Hedden*: The relevant part of Tariff Act of 1886 determined that there is a 10 percent duty on the importation of vegetables, yet the act explicitly excluded from duty importation of fruit. The plaintiff imported tomato and, not surprisingly, claimed that tomato is a fruit, not vegetable. The court rejected his claim. Now, if you look up the word "tomato" in the dictionary, you would be surprised by the court's ruling. The dictionary defines "tomato" as "soft juicy red or yellow *fruit* eaten raw or cooked,"[13] and botanists would probably agree. The same goes for such things as avocados, cucumbers, squash, beans, and peas; botanically, they are classified as fruit. The court, aware of this dictionary definition, says, however, and rightly so, I believe, that "in the common language of the people, . . . all these are vegetables, which are grown in kitchen gardens, and which, whether eaten cooked or raw, are, like potatoes, carrots, parsnips, turnips, beets, cauliflower, cabbage, celery, and lettuce, usually served at dinner in, with, or after, soup, fish or meats which constitute the principal part of the repast, and not like fruits generally, as desert."[14] Legal issues aside, this strange little passage captures something important about language. Concept-words and categories employed in natural language often reflect practical uses, determined by specific interests we have in categorizing objects in certain ways. The category of "fruit" may capture something significant for botanists, and there may well be a sound scientific interest in such a category,

[13] OED.
[14] 149 U.S. 304, 305.

but this does not necessarily capture the "common language of the people," to use the court's expression. Within the realm of our everyday-life interests, tomato is a vegetable. This is just a matter of convention; it's how we use the concept in everyday life. Other communities, of course, could use the concept in different ways, corresponding to different practices they may have (serving tomato as desert, for example). Botanists, of course, may have their own specific interests in such categories, and then the categories would have different extension in *their* dialect. There is nothing wrong with that; no confusion is involved here. (There might have been a confusion here if we thought that words like "vegetable" or "fruit" are natural kind predicates. The court assumes, in effect, that in ordinary language use, these are not natural kinds; that is, even if in some specific scientific contexts such words may be used as natural kinds. This seems to me quite right, and I will have more to say about this in the next chapter.)

In one crucial respect, however, the objection under consideration here is in the right neighborhood. Deep conventions are not as arbitrary as surface conventions in a specific sense: deep conventions tend to emerge as normative responses to social and perhaps psychological aspects of the world that actually require such normative responses. In other words, an explanation of a deep convention is bound to be more closely related to reasons than that of most surface conventions.[15] Consider, yet again, the deep conventions that constitute the practices of playing games. Playing games is probably not something that we just happen to do. It is very easy to imagine a world in which people do not play chess or football or any other particular game that we play. But I think that it would be much more difficult, and in any case, much more remote from us, to think of a world in which people do not play any games whatsoever. It is safe to assume that the inhabitants of a game-less world would have to be very different from us, psychologically, socially, and otherwise. Playing games is a response to deep psychological and sociological aspects of human culture, not a coincidence of history.

[15] In chapter 1 we have already seen that arbitrariness admits of degrees.

But now we are back to the original question: what makes
such normative behavior conventional to begin with? Why are
the norms constituting what counts as playing a game conventions at all if, as I claim, such norms are responses to deep aspects of or our social world, or even human nature? The answer
is basically this: the particular normative responses that constitute deep conventions are *underdetermined* by those needs,
functions, purposes, and so forth that give rise to them. Basically, such rules meet the conditions of conventionality because
the norms that we follow have alternatives that we could have
followed instead, achieving the same purposes or fulfilling the
same functions. In a way, this is the flip side of the translation problem. Natural languages differ considerably, in fact, so
much so that accurate translation is sometimes impossible. But
we do not take such differences in contemporary natural languages as evidence of deep differences between the people who
speak them, and rightly so, I think. We just realize that there
are different ways in which we can adequately respond to the
same needs, purposes, and the like, and that different natural
languages often employ, and thus constitute, different, alternative, reactions. In other words, deep conventions are conventions because their content is underdetermined by the reasons
that account for their existence.

Deep conventions tend to be very elusive because they are
rarely manifest in conventional behavior, or practice, that is
not also governed by surface conventions. People do not play
competitive games in the abstract; they play particular games,
like chess or football, that are constituted by surface conventions. (Although it is worth noting that small children sometimes come close to playing an abstract game, as it were; they
just play something and invent the rules as they go along. It is
almost as if they practice what it is to play a game.) Similarly, in
the ordinary use of language, we employ, for example, certain
linguistic categorizations according to the surface rules of the
relevant natural language, thus instantiating deep conventions
in their surface appearance, so to speak. Deep conventions typically come to our attention only on special occasions, when
there is a problem of translation, or more generally, when a

need to interpret the surface conventions arises. Otherwise, in the ordinary course of events, we just follow the relevant surface conventions.

But if social practices consist of following surface conventions, what makes it the case that deep conventions are *social rules* at all? Consider this example: There is an underlying norm that requires dress codes under certain circumstances, and then there are norms about what counts as the appropriate attire on particular types of occasions. The social practice appears to us in the practice of following the latter norms: What you see when you observe social behavior is the practice of following the surface conventions. But it is still the case that the deep convention is the underlying norm that people follow, albeit indirectly, that is, by following the corresponding surface conventions on the appropriate occasions. (I will return to this example shortly.)

You may object that I am confusing the rule with its underlying reason. There is a reason to have a dress code in certain circumstances, and then conventions determine what counts as complying with this reason on various occasions. This is a captivating account, but it is not accurate.

There are two ways in which reasons underlie the content of norms: reasons can determine the content of the norm, or they can partly determine it. If the reasons fully determine the content of the norm, the norm is not a convention. There is a reason not to torture people, and this reason determines the content of the norm that "It is wrong to torture people." This is not a convention because the norm does not have alternatives that we could have followed instead, still complying with the reason(s) against torture. In this case, the underlying reason completely determines its corresponding norm. But this is not the case with the dress code norm. Suppose that the reasons, or needs, functions, and so forth for having dress code norms in our society are P. Let us assume that P consists in the reasons to show respect for people by some outward appearance. Now, it shouldn't be difficult to imagine a society where P is instantiated by a different kind of social practice, for instance, that people paint their faces in various colors in comparable circumstances (or perhaps they wear feathers, or different sizes of earrings; the possibilities are numerous). And then, of course, if you live in this different society, it would be pointless for you to associate the social functions of P with any particular dress code. This is what makes the underlying norms of dress codes conventional.

In other words, here is how the conventional setting works: in our culture, one way in which we manifest respect for people is by dressing in certain ways on certain occasions. In other societies, the same social function of showing respect on comparable occasions can be practiced by other means, such as painting one's face or wearing feathers. This is the relevant deep convention. But such deep conventions can only be practiced by following their corresponding surface conventions. So there might be a convention that if men attend a wedding, they should wear a suit and a tie. This is how they are expected to manifest the relevant kind of respect for such an occasion. And then this suit and tie norm is the surface convention men would follow on such occasions. And of course there are many other surface conventions that instantiate the same underlying deep convention (i.e., of showing respect by dressing in certain ways).

It may be worth noting that people are often quite aware of the fact that they follow two conventions on such occasions, not one. When you wear a tie to the wedding, you know that you follow the convention to wear a tie, and that's why you put it on, but then you also know that you follow a convention by following such a convention. Perhaps this becomes clearer when you refuse to abide by the convention. You may refuse to put on a tie for the wedding you attend, not because you have any particular aversion to the tie convention, but because you have an objection to the idea of a dress code convention. You may think that the convention to dress up conventionally is not worth following, that is, you basically object to the deep convention, not to its particular manifestation in the relevant surface conventions. As with difficulties in translation, deep conventions tend to come to our attention in cases of deviant behavior, or in those cases in which interpretation is called fore. My history professor at college used to say that when his king was threatened by checkmate, he would simply declare a republic. Taken seriously (which I hope he did not), this is not just a violation of the rules of chess; it is a violation of the deep conventions constituting what counts as playing a competitive game.

How Deep Is "Deep"?

It is not surprising or difficult to see that deep conventions tend to be much more durable than surface conventions. Since deep conventions constitute normative responses to deep aspects of our social lives, they tend to last for a long time, even when the surface conventions that instantiate them change, sometimes quite substantially. Furthermore, though both surface and deep conventions can be codified encyclopedically, typically, only surface conventions tend to be codified legislatively. Deep conventions are organic features of our social world. They need to evolve gradually, in a process of habituation and learning that takes considerable time and practice. Furthermore, as I have indicated earlier, deep conventions tend to emerge as normative responses to social and other needs that are deeply engrained in the world we occupy. It is relatively easy to introduce a change in some surface conventions, institutionally or otherwise. But deep conventions are, by their very nature, much less amenable to change. You can create a new genre of theater, for example, but theater itself, as a social-artistic practice, is not easy to create or just abolish. The underlying deep conventions of theater can change, of course, as they have over the centuries, but those changes are very gradual and span over a considerable amount of time. True, institutions may play a role in gradually eradicating certain deep conventions, mostly by withholding support for the social practices in which such deep conventions manifest themselves. Legislatively codifying deep conventions, however, even if attempted, would rarely succeed.

We should be careful, however, not to take this too far. It may be tempting to think that deep conventions determine something more profound, like the bounds of sense, of what it makes sense to think or say, given the world we live in. But this is clearly too strong. Conventions, as we have seen, are essentially arbitrary rules in the sense that if a rule is a convention, there must be an alternative rule that we could have followed instead, achieving the same purpose, as it were. Thus, even if deep conventions sometimes determine, in a profound way, the ways in which we do things or speak our language, deep conventions are still conventions. If it is possible to conceive of an alternative to the norm that we follow, leaving everything else constant, then the norm cannot be taken to constitute the bounds of what it makes sense to say or think.

Generally speaking, there is a very intimate connection between the fact that a norm is conventional and that it is associated with *contingency, path-dependency,* and *underdeterminacy by reasons.* The arbitrariness of conventions entails that conventional norms are essentially contingent: We could have lived in a world that is, all other things considered, equal to the one we live in, yet followed a different norm, that is, without any significant loss in the purposes, functions, or values that the norm serves for us. In order to know why we happen to follow the conventional norm that we do, typically some story has to be told, a story about the way in which this norm, rather than an alternative one, has come to be practiced. And we can make perfect sense of this contingency and path-dependency by realizing that such norms are underdetermined by reasons.

CHAPTER FOUR

Conventions of Language

Semantics

WHAT aspects of language, and language use, are conventional? This is the question that will be addressed in this and the next chapters. The answer does not purport to be comprehensive. First, I will have nothing to say here about syntax.[1] Second, even within the domains of semantics and pragmatics, which will form the subject of these chapters, my focus will be limited to some key issues. Most of this chapter concentrates on the question of whether the literal meaning of words and linguistic expressions is conventional, and if so, in what sense. In the next chapter we will look at some of the pragmatic aspects of language use, questioning the possible role of conventions in securing communication that is not completely determined by the semantic content of the relevant expression.

If all this looks like an odd task, the impression is not entirely mistaken. Philosophy of language has become extremely

---

[1] The syntax of natural languages is extensively researched by generative linguistics, and the scientific details of this body of research cannot be addressed here. It may be worth noting that there seems to be nothing in the general ideas of generative linguistics that would contradict the basic ideas defended in this book. According to these theories, syntax is roughly divided between the deep, universal, rules of grammar and their surface instantiations in particular languages. The former, it is claimed, does not have any humanly possible alternatives, and hence deep rules of syntax/grammar are not conventions. Conventional variations, differing between natural languages, are present only at the surface.

sophisticated in the last few decades. Its interest in the conventional aspects of language, however, has been rather marginal, at best.[2] Philosophers of language often refer to this or that aspect of language as determined by conventions, but mostly in a context where they feel that no further philosophical analysis is called for. Some of these assumptions, however, need to be questioned. We will see that somewhat less is conventional about language than is usually assumed.

Notation

Natural languages have two main notational aspects.[3] Primary of those is the sound-sense relations. There is no language of any kind without expressions having some determinate senses (or meanings). This is what makes a string of sounds or symbols into a language, that the sounds or symbols stand for expressions that have meanings. Therefore, every language must have some rules connecting the sounds or symbols to the meaning

---

[2] The literature is abundant with expressions like "the conventional meaning of words" and similar formulations. However, in the mainstream of contemporary philosophy of language, the conventionality of literal meaning is not a topic that is frequently addressed. (For example, Ludlow's extensive anthology, *Reading in Philosophy of Language*, containing forty-two contributions, does not have the word "convention" in its index, though it does have "convention T," and "conventional implicatures.") Historically, Wittgenstein was probably the most forthright conventionalist about meaning, though the word "convention" is not one he uses, nor is it clear that he would have thought about conventions in the sense defined by Lewis. J. L. Austin also seems to have assumed that literal meaning is conventional, but his main focus was on the conventional aspect of illocutionary acts. Grice also assumed that literal meaning is conventional. Quine and Davidson explicitly denied the conventionality of language, though for different reasons. Lewis, of course, thought that the sound-sense relations (and some other aspects of language) are conventional, but he did not argue that literal meaning or sense is conventional. Some of the more recent literature will be addressed below.

[3] My use of the word "notation" here is probably broader than its standard meaning in English. I have not managed to find a better word; perhaps the words "signification" could have been used. Hopefully, the text will clarify what I mean.

they express or stand for. Basically, these are rules of the form S [a particular sound] stands for (signifies) M [where M is the literal meaningsense of a word or some other linguistic expression]. Note that sound-sense relations are entirely language-specific. Different sounds in different natural languages may signify the same sense; they have the same literal meaning. (For example, the English word "computer" means exactly the same as "ordinateur" in French, or "mechashev" in Hebrew.)

Written languages have, in addition to these sound-sense rules, another set of rules that determine the script notation of the relevant sounds. As we know, historically, script came later. First there was spoken language, then came script that enabled writing.[4] Thus script is notation on notation, as it were: first we have sounds that stand for senses, and then the sounds can be further symbolized by script. The direction is not only historical. The possibility of script is parasitic on the existence of the sound-sense relations (and much more, of course) already in place.

Both of these sets of rules, sound-sense relations and script, are complex. For example, both sound-sense relations and script tend to have specifications that vary from one population to another, even within the same natural language. In the case of sound-sense relations, these are mostly rules determining appropriate pronunciation of words. In the case of script, these are rules determining appropriate spelling, punctuation, and so on. Second, notation admits of a certain kind of vagueness: there are standard, clear cases of notation (both in sound and script), and then there is a range of variations on sounds or symbols that are recognized as such, namely, as usable variations. However, the borderline between usable, or recognizable, variations and those that fall outside this range is typically fuzzy.[5] Finally, a complication that I will largely ignore here, concerns the fact that notation of sound-sense relations is

---

[4] In fact, there still are quite a number of indigenous languages without script.

[5] For those of us who speak English with a foreign accent, these boundaries are sometimes all to vivid, yet often perplexing.

sometimes closely tied with pronunciation-meaning. A familiar case is when vocal emphasis on a certain part of the expression has a different meaning, conveys different content, than an emphasis on a different part.[6] And sometimes this is more subtle, as when vocal variations insinuate what kind of expression was intended, say, whether something was said ironically or not. It is very difficult to determine in the abstract whether such vocal aspects of communication are conventional in nature or not. I presume that this is partly an empirical question.

In spite of these and other complexities, however, the notational aspect of language is very much on the surface. Notation is entirely parasitic on semantics and syntax. Consider the sound-sense relations. Sound-sense relations, as we noted, are always specific to particular natural languages. The linguistic expression in English "The grass is green" basically *means the same* as the equivalent expression in Hungarian "A fú zöld" or, in Hebrew, "Hadeshe yarok," and so on. Different sound-symbols stand for the same sense. Thus, probably the least controversial aspect of this discussion about the conventionality of language is that rules of notation are conventions.[7] In fact, by large, such rules are coordination conventions along the lines suggested by Lewis. Notation is basically a normative solution to a large-scale recurrent coordination problem. As long as we bear in mind that notation is distinct from semantics (and syntax), there are no real difficulties with this suggestion. There is no doubt that in using notation we follow norms. And it is easy to see—as the differences between natural languages and idiolects attest—that those norms are arbitrary in the requisite sense. It is equally clear that the norms of notation solve a coordination problem for the relevant population. In this we

---

[6] E.g., consider the difference between "he *walked* to the market" and "he walked to *the market*."

[7] Laurence, in "The Chomskian Alternative to Convention-Based Semantics," seems to deny this; but, as far as I can tell, most of his argument is actually about semantics and syntax, not really about the notational aspect of language, viz. the sound-sense relation conventions. See also Millikan, "Language Conventions Made Simple." Whether Millikan's account is at odds with the thesis I advance here is something that I find very difficult to determine.

should not assume, of course, that first we come to grasp the meaning of a word and then we face a coordination problem of what sound to associate with the meaning. As a general pattern, that would be implausible. Something like this happens with naming: first we gain acquaintance with an object (say, a baby born or a newly discovered star) and then we search for a name to attach to it. But most words do not come to be used by such an explicit process of naming. Presumably, notation and sense come into existence concomitantly, as it were, in a complicated social process. What that process is we need not try to uncover here. Suffice it to say that the idea of a coordination convention provides the rationale of norms of notation; it explains what kind of norms they are and what kind of reasons people have for following the norms. It is not generally a condition of such an explanation that the relevant population must be aware of the coordination problem and self-consciously seek a solution to it by introducing a convention.

The Meaning of Words

Many philosophers assume (or, write as if they assume) that the literal meaning of words we use in a natural language is something that is, by and large, conventionally determined. The assumption seems natural if we focus on the normative aspect of meaning: in using words correctly we follow linguistic norms. Those norms determine what counts as correct use(s) of words (and other expressions). And then when we think about the fact that there are typically different ways of expressing the same idea or the same content, even within the same language, these norms look very much like conventions. I want to argue here that this view is at least partly mistaken. The literal meaning of many, if not most, words in a natural language is not, basically, conventional. I will argue that in most cases the core of literal meaning is not a matter of conventions; conventions only determine the boundaries of literal meaning, what I will call here their extension-range. But before we get to any of this, some conceptual assumptions need to be explicated.

Following current philosophical analysis, I will assume here that the literal meaning of words and sentences should be distinguished from what the sentence/expression means/says in a particular context of utterance (roughly, its semantic content), and from what the speaker means to express in that context. More precisely, perhaps, we can say that (*a*) literal meaning needs to be distinguished from (*b*) the semantic content of an expression/sentence relative to a context of utterance, (*c*) the assertive content of an utterance in the context of speech, namely, the proposition(s) asserted/stated by the speaker in the specific context and, finally, (*d*) further communicative content that the speaker is committed to by uttering the expression in the specific context, which may include, for example, conversational implicatures, presuppositions, and perhaps other content that is obviously and transparently entailed by what has been said in the specific context of the utterance.[8] Admittedly, these distinctions, though widely used, are rather controversial in the literature. Different writers draw the lines differently, often driven by particular theoretical interests that make one kind of distinction more useful than another. I do not wish to take sides in any of these controversies. For our purposes, the essential point to keep in mind is that literal meaning is basically fixed by the rules of language, whereas the other aspects of linguistic communication are often context sensitive.

A brief clarification of this conceptual framework should suffice here. Let us begin with the distinction between the literal meaning of words and the semantic content of their use in specific speech-contexts. The semantic content of an expression relative to a context is basically a combination of what is contributed to the content of communication by the literal meaning of the words/sentences uttered and objective features of the utterance, such as who is speaking, time, place, and other relevant contextual facts. Probably the least controversial example of the distinction can be given by considering pure indexicals

[8] In fact, we may add another layer here concerning the kind of action that is sometimes performed by the relevant speech. This will be discussed in the next chapter.

(e.g. "I," "now," "today," "next week"). If the speaker says "I will go to the cinema today," what has been said is partly determined by the literal meaning of the words used, and partly by the objective referent of "I" and "today." The question of whether demonstratives (like "he," "you," "that," "this," etc.) work in a similar way is rather controversial and I will not go into this here.[9] Intuitively, however, the idea is that the meaning of a sentence in a context of utterance is sometimes a combination of the literal meaning of the words used and some objective features of the utterance that together determine what *the sentence says* in the relevant context.

In addition to the semantic content of the utterance, in order to understand what the speaker has asserted, further contextual background may be required. In other words, the assertive content of an expression may depend on specific contextual background, knowledge of which is shared by speaker and hearer. Consider, for example, possessive ascriptions: Suppose a speaker says, "I just finished reading Hilary's book." In order to know what has been asserted here, one would need to know whether "Hilary's book" refers to a book that Hilary wrote, or a book that belongs to her, or maybe a book about her. Under normal circumstances, the content of such expressions is specified by the context of the utterance, knowledge of which is shared by speaker and hearer. Without this contextual background it is impossible to determine what has been asserted.

Finally, it is widely agreed that the content of an assertion can go substantially beyond what has been explicitly said/asserted. Let's call it the implied content of the utterance. Roughly, then, the implied content of S in context C can be defined as the content that the speaker, in the specific context of C, is committed to by uttering S, and that the hearers are expected to know that the speaker is committed to, and the speaker can be expected to know this. Thus, in addition to what has been explicitly said by an utterance, it might contain what is conversationally implicated by it, what is presupposed by it, and perhaps other content

---

[9] Kaplan, "Demonstratives"; and cf. Soames, "Direct Reference, Propositional Attitudes, and Semantic Content."

that is obviously and transparently entailed by the utterance in its context of utterance.[10]

For our present purposes, however, the distinction that matters is between literal meaning on the one hand, and semantic/ assertive content on the other. Again, the basic idea here is that literal meaning is fixed by the rules of language, whereas the complete content of an utterance, what has been said, asserted, and implicated by it, may vary with context. This gives rise to the natural assumption that literal meaning is basically determined by the conventions of language about what words and sentences standardly mean. It is this conventional underpinning of literal meaning that I would like to question here. To be sure, I do not think that we have reasons to doubt that literal meaning is basically normative, constituted by the rules of language. The question is whether these constitutive rules are, by and large, conventions. And this, of course, depends on whether they are *arbitrary* in the requisite sense. So let us look at some difficulties here. First, we need a clear sense of what the conventionality of literal meaning would require. Thus, suppose the claim is that the rules, R_m, determining what a word, P, literally means in a natural language L, are conventions; then the following conditions have to obtain:

In using the word P,

1. the population of L-users normally follow R_m in circumstances C;
2. there is a reason, or combination of reasons, A, for L-users to follow R_m in circumstances C;
3. there is at least one other set of rules, R_m^*, that if members of L-users had actually followed in circumstances C, then A would have been a sufficient reason for members of L-users to follow R_m^* instead of R_m in circumstances C, and at least partly because R_m^* is the set of rules generally followed instead of R_m.

The rules R_m and R_m^* are such that it is impossible (or pointless) to comply with both of them concomitantly in circumstances C.

---

[10] See, for example, Soames, "Drawing the Line."

I am not assuming here that we can actually formulate precise rules that would capture the literal meaning of words in a natural language. And I am certainly not assuming here that in learning to speak a language we learn how to apply general rules; nothing of what I say here bears on the processes by which people acquire language competency. As I have argued in the previous chapter, however, the use of words (and other expressions) in a natural language is a norm-governed activity; those norms constitute how speakers of the language are to use the words, and sometime they use a word incorrectly, in which case they might be corrected by competent speakers, saying, "This is not what P really means," or "This is not how P is used," and so forth. In other words, I take it as nonproblematic to assume that the literal meaning of words is determined by norms that specify correct and incorrect uses of the words.[11]

Condition 2 may require some clarification; what can be reasons for following rules such as R_m? It may seem awkward to suggest that we follow rules that determine the literal meaning of words for some reasons. But in fact, no mystery is involved here. There are concrete reasons for having the words of a natural language that we do. For instance, we use proper names in order to be able to refer to people or locations; we have specific reasons, grounded in logic, for having words for logical connectives; scientific reasons for using words referring to natural kinds and such; psychological and social reasons for having words expressing emotions, sentiments, and so on. Generally, the use of words serves rather specific functions, needs, or purposes in our lives, and those functions constitute the reasons for having this or that word in a language. Thus, the idea that the rules determining the literal meaning of words we use are supported by reasons should not be seen as particularly problematic

---

[11] Perhaps this is one of the main points of Wittgenstein's famous remarks on rule following in §§143–242, particularly §§198–201 of his *Philosophical Investigations*. If so, one may think that Kripke's skeptical interpretation of these remarks amounts to a skeptical argument about the very possibility of the determination of meaning by rules (see Kripke, *Wittgenstein on Rules and Private Language*). This is a very complicated debate into which I do not want to enter.

or mysterious. It is tantamount to the platitude that what words mean in a natural language is largely determined by the relevant purposes or functions of using language in the various contexts of communication and thought.

The crucial element pertains to the third condition. In order to show that rules constituting literal meaning are by and large conventional, we would need to show that condition 3 generally applies. But it is very doubtful, in numerous cases, that it does. There are several categories of words that should immediately raise suspicion: logical connectives, natural kind predicates, first-person pronoun, and so on. In all these cases, we have norms for using words, norms that determine their literal sense/meaning, but in a way that does not seem to admit of any genuine alternatives, as required by condition 3. For example, isn't it the case that logic *determines* what connectives such as conjunction or material implication literally mean? Is it not the case that when we use a natural kind predicate, we just assume that it is the real nature of the thing referred to that *determines* what it is, and thus, determines what the word literally means? And can we really conceive of, say, a first-person pronoun that is somehow different from the way we use the word "I" in English? (To be sure: this is not suggested as an argument, I'm just posing the question here.)

An affirmative answer to the question of conventionality of literal meaning might be thought to be supported by the profound practice-dependence of literal meaning. There are two related points here, and I would like to respond before we proceed. First, it is conceivable to have a language that does not have certain concept-words that most languages do. Perhaps there is a language that can do without, say, some demonstratives. Perhaps it would be a flawed language, one that does not allow its speakers to express certain thoughts and ideas that we can. But a language it may be. Nevertheless, none of this would show that the meaning of such words is conventional. A norm does not become conventional just because some population can do without it.[12]

---

[12] Consider this rather extreme example: there is a hunter-gatherer tribe in the Amazons, called Piraha, which has a very unusual language—for instance,

Second, it may be thought that norms determining the literal meaning of words must be conventional, since reasons to follow those norms are compliance-dependent. People cannot use a word unless the word forms part of an actual language, that is, unless it is used in the same way by others in the relevant linguistic community. In other words, there is a very close relationship between the fact that a word literally means P, and the fact that there is a linguistic community that actually uses the word to mean P. Without the linguistic practices of a certain community, a word cannot have the literal meaning that it does. Surely this is correct. But we must be cautious here. As we noted earlier, not every kind of practice dependent reason is indicative of conventionality. There are many things it would be pointless for us to do unless others do it as well. General compliance with a norm often forms part of the conditions for the successful realization of the norm's action guiding function. This is certainly the case with conventional norms, but not exclusively. A norm is conventional, however, if and only if there is also an alternative norm that could have served the relevant population in the relevant circumstances just as well. Whether this is the case with literal meaning of words remains to be seen.

Let's look at this from a different angle. Surely, one could have thought, at least the meaning of words that stand for conventional practices are conventionally determined. So consider a word that signifies a conventional practice, like playing chess: is *the meaning* of the word "chess" a matter of convention? It seems to me that the answer is no. The game, that is, the *activity* of playing chess, is constituted and regulated by conventions. But what would be conventional about having a

---

the Piraha language seems not to have words for color perceptions at all, and more interestingly, it does not have number concepts beyond three. (A fascinating description of this language was published in the *New Yorker*, April 17, 2007, 118–37.) Now, of course, the fact that there is a language that does not have concept-words for numbers does not entail that our number concepts are conventional. See also Rosch, "Natural Categories" (describing research on members of Dani tribe in Indonesia, who also have no color perception words; the research showed, among other things, that they can be taught to understand color perceptions in spite of the fact that none exist in their native tongue).

word that signifies, or stands for, this game/activity? If there is
a reason to have a word that stands for chess, the reason *basically* determines how speakers of the language are to use the
word; namely, to signify the conventional activity of playing
chess. Nothing arbitrary about that (except the notation, that
is, the sound-sense relations, of course). Now, I have italicized
the word "basically" in the previous sentence because there
is a crucial caveat here. It is very easy to imagine a language
that differentiates, say, official chess, as played in tournaments, from chess played by amateurs. So let us assume that
in this language, there are actually two words used, call them
"o-chess" and "a-chess." No doubt, this would be a matter of
convention.

The problem is that we seem to have conflicting intuitions
here: On the one hand, there seems to be nothing conventional
about the basic meaning/sense of most of the words we use.
If there is a certain activity, say, of playing a board game of a
kind, then we need a word to stand for that activity. We call it
"chess." The notation (viz., sound-sense relation) is conventional, of course, but not the literal meaning of the word. The
fact that the reference of the concept-word is a conventional
practice does not render the literal meaning of the relevant
word conventional. (Unless the conventional reference fully
determines the meaning of the word, which is the main exception that I will discuss below.) On the other hand, it seems
equally clear that there is a great deal about the meaning of
words we use that is conventionally determined. As we noted
in the previous chapter, at least some of the more interesting
differences between the meaning of words in different natural
languages would attest to that. Thus, we a need a distinction
here, one that would capture the distinction between the part
of literal meaning that is conventional and the part that is not.

One natural suggestion would be to draw the distinction between different kinds or classes of words or expressions. Perhaps the literal meaning of some words is not conventional, and
of others, it is. To some extent, this is true. It is the case that
the literal meaning of some words is purely conventional (and
I will discuss some examples later.) But as a general solution to

the problem, this distinction would not work. The example of
chess that I just gave here could attest to the difficulty: there is
an activity, conventionally constituted, of playing chess. Now,
the fact that there is a word in English (or any other language,
for that matter) that stands for this type of activity, in itself, does
not seem to be a matter of convention. On the other hand, it is
easy to imagine a language that would draw some distinctions
that are not present in English (e.g., the example of o-chess and
a-chess). And this, surely, might be a matter of convention. So
it does not seem to be the case that we can simply divide the
words of a natural language into the kinds that are conventional
and those that are not; rather, it seems that some elements or
aspects of literal meaning are conventional and others are not.

Vagueness, I believe, provides an important clue to the relevant
distinction here. Consider the extension of a vague predicate,
say, some color word like "blue." Now, some color perceptions
are within the definite extension of "blue" (namely, they are
clearly, undoubtedly blue, if anything is), some are within the
definite nonextension of "blue" (say, yellow, red, and anything
else that is clearly not blue), and there is a range of borderline
cases that may or may not be "blue." If X is a borderline case of
"blue," then there is a sense in which it would not be a mistake
to classify X as blue and it would not be a mistake to classify it as
not blue. However, there are contexts in which further specifications are possible. Borderline cases can be eliminated to some
extent in a given context; so that X can *be regarded as* blue in a
context even if it is a borderline case in a different context.[13]
And, crucially, some of these specifications can be conventional.
Consider, for example, a community/dialect of artists; naturally,
they would need much finer distinctions of color perceptions
than most of us need in our everyday lives. Thus in the artists'
idiolect, X might not be blue at all, even if X is a borderline case
in our ordinary language. To be sure, I am not suggesting that
the reasons artists have for drawing finer distinctions *determine*
that X is not blue (how could they?); the reasons only require

[13] See Soames, *Understanding Truth*, chap. 7, and Soames, "Higher-Order
Vagueness for Partially Defined Predicates."

some fine-grained distinctions; how exactly those distinctions
are made is often just a matter of convention.

So here is the suggested distinction I have in mind. The basic
or core meaning of a vague predicate (or any other word, for that
matter) is determined by its application to its definite extension
(and definite non-extension). Now, the idea is that basic meaning
is generally not a matter of convention. The reasons for having a
word with a certain literal meaning, *determine* the definite extension (and definite non-extension) of the word. Therefore, the
norms that constitute the literal meaning of a word as it applies
to its definite extension (and definite non-extension) are, mostly,
not conventions. However, conventions can specify borderline
cases and include them in the extension or non-extension under certain conditions or in some specific contexts. As we just
noted, it is easy to imagine languages or idiolects that vary with
respect to the extension of "blue" and these variances can be conventional. Here's another simple example: in most places, the
word "evening" is applied only to, roughly, around six to nine
o'clock. Earlier in the day it is "afternoon" and later it is "night."
In other places (Chicago, for one), it is perfectly okay to say
"good evening" at 4:00 p.m. Surely, these differences are purely
conventional. However, note that there is a necessary overlap.
Unless it is the case that, say, 8:00 p.m. is "evening" in both idiolects (say, that of New York City and Chicago), the word would
not have been the same word in English. The definite extension
is essential to what the word "evening" means. Languages and
idiolects can vary, however, with respect to specifications of their
extension-range. And the latter is, often, a matter of conventions.
One conspicuous difference between natural languages concerns
cases where equivalent concept-words have different ranges of
application. One language, for example, may have a word cover-
ing cases of a, b, c, and d, whereas in another language, the corresponding word would only cover a, b, and c, and then a different
word would be used to refer to cases of type d. Such differences
are, typically, conventional.[14]

---

[14] These cases explain the rather striking difference between the number of
words different languages have. English, for example, contains about a quarter

Now, I believe that this simple model can be extended to cover more complicated cases. Consider, for example, a word like "art," or "works of art." The application range of "art" can vary considerably between cultures and languages, as it certainly has varied over the centuries in Western culture. At least some of these variations and differences are due to different social conventions that determine what art is in different cultures. These differences are bound to affect the range of objects that the word "art" or "work of art" applies to. Consequently, there is no doubt that the literal meaning of "art" would reflect these conventional differences. What is not conventional, however, is the core of meaning. Even in the case of "art," there is a range of objects within the definite extension of the word that remains constant across time and cultural variances. If this condition does not obtain, there would be no justification for thinking that "art" in one language or idiolect should be translated to "art" in the other. In other words, if we use the same concept-word despite substantial variations in the conventional range of its application, such use would be warranted only if there is a certain core range of application that remains constant across variations. (You might object that if "art" is a *family resemblance* concept, this condition does not have to obtain. I'll get to this in a moment.) And if there is such a core of cases, then having a word for it does not seem to be a matter of convention. Now, it is certainly true that the meaning of some words has changed so much that they no longer refer to the same thing(s), even in the core range of applications. In such cases, however, the appropriate conclusion should be that it is no longer the same word; it now has *a different literal meaning*. Sound is the same, but the sense associated with the sound simply changed.[15]

---

of a million words in common usage; Hebrew, only about a 100,000, probably less. Most European languages are somewhere in between; it is estimated that French has about 125,000.

[15] For example, the word "meat," used these days to refer to the edible flesh of animals, meant, some centuries ago, basically what the word "food," in general, means today. (Meat comes from the Old English word "mete," which meant "food.") Thus, for example, apples would have been within the definite extension of "meat" at the time, whereas now apple is in the definite

Note that this analysis allows us to talk about degrees of conventionality of literal meaning. The literal meaning of some words can be more conventional than that of others. The degree of conventionality would be a function of the proportion between the word's core extension and its conventionally variant extension-range. In the case of "art," for example, the core is very limited compared with its variant, conventional extensions. The literal meaning of "art" in this respect is, indeed, much more conventional than of many other words. For example, I think it would be safe to assume that the word signifying the first-person pronoun has little conventional variance, its literal meaning hardly conventional at all.

Now, perhaps at this point you may think that I have contradicted myself: have I not claimed earlier that forms of art are constituted by *deep conventions*? If it is the case, as I have argued in the previous chapter, that there are some deep conventions that constitute what certain forms or art (theater, poetry, etc.) consist of, then would it not be the case that even the core or basic meaning of "art" (or "theater," etc.) is conventional? There is no contradiction here. As I have pointed out above, in relation to the meaning of a word like "chess," the fact that a word stands for a conventional activity does not necessarily render the literal meaning of the word conventional. The game of chess, the activity of playing it by the rules that constitute it, is conventional. But this does not entail that having a word that signifies this activity is, in itself, a mater of conventions. The same point applies to deep conventions. The fact that there is a type of activity that is constituted by deep conventions (e.g., playing games, or creating works of art) does not render the literal meaning of words that signify them conventional. Generally speaking, the conventionality of the meaning of a word in a natural language does not depend on the nature of the practice that is signified by the word; it depends on the question of whether the reasons

nonextension of "meat." I think that the natural conclusion here is that the literal meaning of the word "meat" simply changed over the centuries; it no longer means "food" but only a specific subset of "food." Sound is the same, but the literal meaning of this word has changed.

for having such a word in the relevant language determine its core meaning. Hence the conclusion is actually the opposite of what the objection assumes: precisely because there are some deep conventions that constitute a certain type of activity and its conceptualization, there are reasons to signify the activity in question, and thus the literal meaning of the word that stands for this type of activity is not, in its core, a matter of conventions. Conventional variances of meaning, as we have seen, are certainly possible, when further specification of literal meaning is called for. In this, however, words like "game" or "art" are not different from any other vague concept-word.[16]

The role of deep conventions in language is different: deep conventions typically constitute conceptual classifications, they generate conventional taxonomies of various aspects of the world or our social activities. Thus, for example, deep conventions may constitute a form of art that is instantiated by specific surface conventions people follow under the circumstances. Or they may constitute certain general types of activities, like playing (competitive) games or such (which are then instantiated by the surface conventions of particular games). In all these cases, however, what the deep conventions constitute is not the literal meaning of the word that signifies them, but a general type of activity and its corresponding conceptualization. Deep conventions constitute, as it were, the *reference* of the words that signify them, not their literal meaning/sense. In using such a word as, say, "game," we actually refer to the deep conventions that constitute games in or culture, but this does not entail that the literal meaning of "game" is conventional. On the contrary, the meaning of "game" is basically determined by the reasons for having a word that signifies the type of activity in question.

Let me reiterate the main point here since it is quite important. There are numerous words in a natural language that refer

[16] Remember that vagueness admits of degrees; some words can be more vague than others, that is, in having a larger range of borderline cases. "Art" is probably much more vague than, say, "chair" or "automobile." This, I believe, stems partly from the complexity of the practice we call art, and partly from conventional variances between cultures that tend to specify the extension range of artistic practices.

to conventional practices. Many of these conventional practices, as we have seen in the previous chapter, instantiate deep
conventions. Therefore, there is often something profoundly
conventional in the practices and their corresponding concep-
tualizations that words refer to (or signify, or stand for). The
conventional nature of the reference, however, does not necessarily entail that the literal meaning of the word that signifies it
is, in itself, a matter of convention. There is no need for a convention to refer to a convention (except as a notational device,
of course, like the sound-sense relation). The literal meaning
of such words, at least as it applies to their definite extension,
is determined by the need to refer to the relevant conventional
practice that the word signifies.

A GENUINE AND SOME PUTATIVE EXCEPTIONS

One might object that there are many exceptions to the general
idea that is presented in the previous section. Indeed, there are
some genuine exceptions, I will argue, but much fewer than
one would have thought. Let me begin with a genuine exception and then consider some other cases.

Single Criterion Words

The idea that the core of literal meaning is not, generally, a
matter of conventions has an important exception: The exception consists in words whose literal meaning is *fully determined
by their conventional reference*. Consider, for example, units of
measurement, say, of distances. There are very good reasons
for using various ways to measure distances and have words that
signify those units. Clearly, however, the reasons for measuring
distance in identifiable units do not determine the particular
units to be used. In fact, as we all know, numerous systems of
measuring distance have been employed over the centuries, and
even today, when global coordination is so important, there are
still two main systems in use, the so called imperial and metric systems. These measurement systems are, of course, purely

conventional.[17] Now, take one of these units, say, the unit of a yard: What the word "yard" means is simply identical with the convention that determines the length of a yard. (Yard, of course, is an arbitrary measurement unit, precisely in the sense of arbitrariness that was defined in chapter 1.) In other words, the reference of "yard," namely, the relevant convention, fully constitutes the meaning of this word, it is identical with its sense. The word simply signifies the convention that constitutes the particular length.

We can call such words *single criterion words*,[18] to emphasize the fact that these are words whose meaning is constituted, and exhausted, by the convention that they signify. Now, if the meaning of a word simply *is* the convention that it signifies, there is a sense in which the literal meaning is conventional. It is, however, a rather unique sense in which meaning is conventional: because these are single-criterion words, the conventionality of the reference carries over, so to speak, to the conventionality of the meaning of the word. The reason for having a word that stands for, say, a yard, is exactly the same reason we have for its reference, namely, the reason for having a measuring unit of this kind. Since the reason for having the unit underdetermines the measurement of it, the norm constituting the unit of a yard is, of course, conventional.

Many of the single-criterion words signify specific conventions within social practices, like games, forms of art, and such. Consider, for example, the word "touchdown" as used in the context of (American) football: the meaning of "touchdown" is fully determined by the conventions of football that determine what counts as a touchdown. The reference of "touchdown" is

---

[17] One might think that the metric system is not really conventional, since the unit of one meter was determined according to a natural distance (one-tenth of a million of half of the longitude of the earth cutting across central Paris). But of course, the choice of this "natural" distance is completely arbitrary. How the meter was actually measured, and how important it was for the French Academy to try to determine the length of a meter by this "natural" distance, is a fascinating story, told in Ken Alder's book *The Measure of All Things*.

[18] I borrow this term from Putnam ("The Meaning of Meaning") but use it somewhat differently.

a convention and the convention fully determines what "touchdown" means. Similarly, of course, the literal meaning of "checkmate" is determined by the relevant convention of chess that constitutes what counts as checkmate in the game.

But now you might wonder, why would the meaning of a word like "checkmate" be conventional, as I claim here, but the meaning of "chess," not so? The distinction resides in the fact that "chess" is not a single-criterion word. As we noted in chapter 2, the social practice of playing chess is not identical with the set of conventions that constitute the game. Chess is a complex social practice, a rather elaborate type of activity, that includes much more than the set of rules that constitute the game. And, as noted above, once there is a certain type of activity, whether conventionally established or not, we would need a word to stand for it, to signify it. There is nothing conventional about that; the reasons for using a word to stand for the activity of playing chess determine what the word literally means (at least with respect to its definite extension).

The idea that some words function very much like a move in a game will be further explored in the next chapter, where we will see that some performative expressions (like "Hi," "thanks," etc.) function in a similar way. They are not exactly single-criterion words, but their meaning is purely conventional, and for very similar reasons; such expressions function like making a move in a conventional social practice, and thus their meaning is basically identical with the conventional "move" that expressing them amounts to.

Family Resemblance

In arguing against the conventionality of literal meaning, I have assumed that conventional variations in what words literally mean in various contexts affect only the extension-range of the word, not its core meaning, that is, its definite extension. However, *family resemblance* concept-words would seem to be an obvious counterexample to this thesis. As Wittgenstein defined the idea of family resemblance concepts, they are words that refer to "phenomena [that] have no one thing in common which makes us use the same word for all,—but they are *related* to one another in many different ways."[19] "Game," "language," and "number" are his famous examples of family resemblance concept-words. Wittgenstein urges us to look at the various cases in which we use the word "game," for example, and see if we can come up with any feature that makes us use the word "game" for all of them. We will not be able to provide such a common feature, he claims. Instead, "we see a complicated network of similarities overlapping and criss-crossing: sometimes overall similarities, sometimes similarities of detail."[20] And, he adds: "I can think of no better expression to characterize these similarities than 'family resemblance'; for the various resemblances between members of a family: build, features, colour of eyes, gait, temperament, etc. etc. overlap and criss-cross in the same way. And I shall say: 'games' form a family."[21]

Family resemblance concepts would indicate that there are concept-words that have no core of definite extension (and definite nonextension) that applies to all the standard uses of the word in the language. If there is not any feature due to which we call various phenomena by the same concept-word, but only vague similarities, as it were, then there is no assurance that the definite extensions of each and every standard use of the word would overlap. Take a word, say, P: in one standard application of P, say, P_X, it covers cases a, b, and c; in another standard application, P_Y, it covers cases a, d, e; and then perhaps in a third application, P_Z, it covers d, e, f. If this is possible, as the idea of family resemblance clearly suggests, then the X and Z applications of P would have no extension in common. Nevertheless, Wittgenstein suggests, it is perfectly okay to use the word P to apply to both, that is, without ambiguity, figurative speech, or any other nonstandard meaning involved. Furthermore, Wittgenstein's concrete examples of family resemblance concept-words seems to suggest that this is not an esoteric phenomenon; perhaps as common to words we use in a natural language as vagueness.

[19] Wittgenstein, *Philosophical Investigations*, §65.
[20] Ibid., §66.
[21] Ibid., §67.

I think that we should seriously doubt that there are family resemblance concepts, or at least we should doubt that they are as common as Wittgenstein suggests. To begin with, the examples are not quite convincing. Take "game," for instance. Undoubtedly, "game" is a vague concept: it has many debatable borderline cases. But is it also a family resemblance concept-word? In the previous chapter, discussing the deep conventions of games, I argued at some length that games do have a great deal in common. They are typically rule-governed (even if the rules are rudimentary, tentative, or in flux); the rules constitute what counts as winning (and losing), or at least, what counts as success in the game; games concern artificial interactions, with a certain element of detachment from real-life concerns; and they normally involve a certain demarcation of participants distinguished from nonparticipants. (And there may be other similar features.) Notably, none of this is convincingly refuted by Wittgenstein's examples. For instance, he doubts that every game necessarily involves winning or losing, and he even doubts that games are necessarily rule governed. But again, Wittgenstein's counterexample—"a child throws his ball at the wall and catches it again"—is not convincing. The game of a child bouncing the ball at the wall is, perhaps, a borderline case; it is a rudimentary form of a game. Nevertheless, there are rules here: after all, the point of this game is to catch the ball bouncing back from the wall; and the rule defines a criterion of success—you win if you catch, and lose if you don't. Furthermore, even a child normally understands that there is a difference between playing with the ball by bouncing it against the wall, and throwing the ball at his sibling's head. Seeing the child doing the latter, we normally tell him, "Careful, this is not a game!" And we expect (even) children to understand this.

Be this as it may, the main problem is not the examples. The problem is that there is an inherent difficulty in the very idea of family resemblance concepts. The problem stems from the profound indeterminacy of similarity relations. Similarity between instances of a word's application cannot possibly explain why we use the same word to cover them all, because there is always an indefinite number of possible similarities, and we would need some idea of which similarities are relevant and essential to the meaning of the word. Seeing two people punching each other (and perhaps a crowd watching, etc.), how could you tell whether it is a boxing game or a real fight? After all, they are very similar. Surely, boxing resembles a real fight much more than it resembles tennis or golf! What makes it a game, then? Of course we do know the answer; because boxing is rule-governed, the rules determine what counts as winning or losing, and so on. It is *this* similarity that matters, but we only know that it matters because we know what is essential to, or characteristic of, "games," and what is not.

Similarity, in other words, is always relative to certain criteria of relevance. It makes little sense to suggest that X and Y are instances of "games" just because there is a resemblance between them; almost every pair of objects one can think of would have some aspects that are similar; it is always crucial to know in what respect a similarity matters and why.[22] The White House and my house are both "houses," though they are really not very similar. Both resemble a box of cigarettes (white, rectangular. etc.), but even a gigantic cigarette box is not a house. What makes us use the same word for the White House and my house is that there is a feature in common to both that makes us use the word "house" for them, namely, that they are constructions designed for humans to live in them and can function in that way.[23] The relation of "similarity" or "resemblance" is just too indeterminate to explain why we use words in the ways we do. This is not to deny, however, that the defining features of words we use—features that make us use

---

[22] Note that this is a logical-epistemic point, *not a psychological one.* I take no stance here on issues pertaining to the mental processes by which we normally categorize perceived objects or ways in which we actually grasp similarities. In other words, I do not need to deny that some kinds of similarities are perhaps more natural than others, or that there is some psychological grounding of salience, etc. I am raising some doubts here about Wittgenstein's philosophical insight, not about his psychological assumptions.

[23] A "doll-house or a "house of cards" is not really a house. We often use language in a derivative or figurative way. This is not what Wittgenstein relies upon.

the same word for its various applications—are not vague. On
the contrary, such defining features tend to be vague and would
normally have borderline cases. This is what makes it generally impossible to provide precise definitions of the meaning of
words in terms of a set of necessary and sufficient conditions.
Vagueness, however, does not entail family resemblance.

Let me summarize: I don't think that it is provable that there
are no family resemblance concepts. Language is extremely
flexible.[24] However, I did try to argue that if there is such a phenomenon, it is much more esoteric than Wittgenstein would
have us believe. Most concept-words we use in our language
have a range of definite extension (and definite nonextension)
because there usually is a certain feature, or number of features,
that those instances have in common and that make us use the
same word for all. And those features are typically not arbitrary.
They instantiate the reasons for having the relevant word in
our language, and those reasons typically determine the word's
application to its definite extension. Hence I suggest that it is
generally the case that the literal meaning of a word applied to
its definite extension is not conventional. Conventional variations, I have suggested, mostly concern the extension range of
potentially borderline cases or other distinctions in the extension range that are not essential to the core of meaning.

Natural Kinds

Consider now another potential class of words that might be an
exception to the idea suggested here, though from the opposite
angle. It might be thought that *natural kind* words would not
admit of conventional variations in their extension range. After

---

[24] For a view of this issue that is more sympathetic to Wittgenstein, see Baker
and Hacker, *Wittgenstein, Meaning and Understanding*, chap. 10. I find their arguments in defense of Wittgenstein's position somewhat weak, however, because
the contrast they draw is between family resemblance concepts and words that
can be defined by what they call *Merkmal*-definition, namely, a conjunction of
characteristic marks that form necessary and sufficient conditions. I doubt that
this is a genuine dichotomy. The impossibility of providing a *Merkmal*-defini-
tion for a word does not entail that the word is a family resemblance one.

all, the idea of a natural kind word is that we intend to refer to some aspect of the world, whatever *it really is*, or turns out to be.[25] Hence it might seem that natural kinds do not really admit of any conventional variations in their range of extension. The extension is fully determined by reality, as it were. But this is not quite accurate. Our use of words in natural language is partly determined by the kind of interests we have in the relevant context of use. Often our interest in a given speech context employing a natural kind predicate has very little to do with scientific or metaphysical accuracy. Recall the example of tomatoes from *Nix v Hedden*: even if tomatoes are, scientifically speaking, fruit and not vegetable (assuming there is scientific grounding for such taxonomies), regarding them as vegetable in our everyday discourse makes perfect sense. That is so, because our interest in such classification is normally a culinary one, not scientific. Similarly, the label on a bottle of mineral water indicating that it is "pure water" is not necessarily false advertising, even if there is more in the bottle that H_2O. The appropriate extension of words we use is often context sensitive, partly determined by our practical interests. Admittedly, this is mostly a pragmatic issue, determined by specific contexts of utterance. For example, ordering a bottle of water in a café is a context in which it is clear to speaker and waiter that the request refers to a bottle that contains *mostly* H_2O, not exclusively. However, in some cases, recurring interests under certain type of circumstances may crystallize into conventions and partly determine the extension of the word in a certain context, that is, as a matter of convention. The example of tomatoes as vegetables might be a case in point.[26]

Proper Names

Let me say a few words on proper names: Proper names are different and somewhat idiosyncratic. On the one hand, our

[25] Putnam, "The Meaning of 'Meaning.'"

[26] Whether this necessarily engenders an ambiguity in the meaning of the relevant word is a question I would like to leave open. Sometimes, I think, it may.

use of proper names seems to be very conventional; there is hardly anything more arbitrary, as it were, then the names we use to refer to individuals or places. On the other hand, there is a sense in which it is very doubtful that proper names are conventions and doubtful that they have a literal meaning at all.

Consider the name of an individual person, say, Ronald Dworkin. He is called Ronald because, I presume, his parents gave him that name. It is not a convention that we use this name to refer to (the person) Ronald Dworkin. To be sure, there is a *conventional practice* of referring to people by names and not, say, by a number or their date of birth, but the name itself is not a convention. It was actually given to Dworkin by his parents and passed down to us from mouth to ear, as it were. In many respects, names very much resemble conventions; for instance, in their arbitrariness. Ronald's parents could have given him any number of other names. But somehow it does not seem quite right to suggest that individuals' names *are* conventions. It is not a convention to use the words "Ronald Dworkin" to refer to the philosopher Ronald Dworkin. Again, the relevant convention here is in the background, that is, the social convention of naming and referring to people by their names.[27] In fact, it is not one convention but a whole set of conventions constituting a social practice. For example, the conventional practice of naming includes certain conventions about how (and who gets) to introduce a name in this or that context, how to announce it to the world, so to speak, what constraints apply to the kind of names that can be used, and so forth. So there is, undoubtedly, a whole practice in our culture, conventionally established, of naming people, places, and the like. But the name itself, that is, the fact—be it a social fact, recurring with some generality—that we use the

---

[27] Admittedly, in some unusual circumstances, conventions can evolve that change a name, mostly of places, rarely of people. Sometimes, for instance, a memorable event happens somewhere, and people start referring to the place by reference to that event; gradually, such repeated use can evolve into a convention that creates a new name for the place, one that is conventionally conferred. But such cases are rather exceptional.

name "Ronald Dworkin" to refer to the relevant person, is not a convention.[28]

Let me sum up the argument: it was suggested that the literal meaning of words we use in a natural language is typically a combination of elements that are not conventional and elements that are conventions. The core of meaning, the word's application to its definite extension, is typically not constituted by conventions. The fact that we have a word literally meaning something is usually explicable, and determined, by the specific needs or functions that the word serves in the language, namely, of referring to some thing(s) that it is useful to refer to. Sometimes, these specific functions exhaust the literal meaning of the word.[29] Mostly, however, words tend to acquire conventional extensions further specifying the literal meaning of the word in certain contexts. Such conventional extensions can vary a great deal, and hence we can speak of degrees of conventionality. The literal meaning of some words can be more conventional than that of others, depending on the proportion between the word's core extension and its conventionally variant extension; the greater the relative conventional variations, the more conventional literal meaning is. We have noted that proper names are somewhat idiosyncratic, in that the relevant conventional practice is at the background, enabling us to use names to refer to people, places, and so on, but a name itself is not a convention. Finally, we have seen that there are certain types of words in a natural language, mostly single-criterion words, whose meaning is basically conventional.

---

[28] This may not be unrelated to the fact that there is a sense in which proper names have no literal meaning. Names, as such, literally mean nothing at all. In some languages, it is conventional to name people using words that actually do have regular meanings (in Hebrew, for instance, people can be called by such words as "pretty," or "brave," etc.). But here, of course, the meaning of the word is not the meaning of the name; it is just borrowed, so to speak, mostly for symbolic purposes. When the word functions *as a name* of an individual, it is still the case, I think, that it has no literal meaning. An exception is the case of partially descriptive names, like "Lake Michigan" or "New York City." For an analysis of partially descriptive names, see Soames, *Beyond Rigidity*, 87–95.

[29] I assume that this may be the case with, e.g., logical connectives, first-person pronouns, some scientific concepts, etc.

CHAPTER FIVE

Conventions of Language

Pragmatics

THERE are two separate issues that form the subject of this chapter. Both of them concern familiar questions about the pragmatic aspects of linguistic communication. In the first part I consider the question of whether there are conventional implicatures. The second part focuses on the role of conventions in performative speech acts.

ARE THERE PRAGMATIC CONVENTIONS?

The main question addressed here is this: What is the role conventions play in securing linguistic communication when the content of an utterance goes beyond what has been explicitly said? Grice's remarkably influential theory of implicatures still provides the main framework of analysis of such cases, and the following discussion will not be an exception. Grice's main insight, I take it, is that our ability to understand content of expressions beyond their semantic/assertive[1] content is due to a combination of two kinds of factors: general norms of conversation that apply to the relevant speech situation, and specific contextual knowl-

---

[1] The question of beyond what, exactly, conversational implicatures operate is somewhat controversial. Grice typically speaks about the distinction between what is said and what is implicated; presumably, by "what is said," Grice includes assertive (and not just semantic) content. Scott Soames, however, argues that a great deal of assertive content is also partly determined by pragmatic features of conversation, including implicatures. See Soames, "Drawing the Line."

edge that is shared by speaker and hearer in the circumstances of the utterance. In normal conversational situations, when the main purpose of speech is the cooperative exchange of information, there are certain general maxims that apply. Grice helpfully enlisted and classified these maxims of ordinary conversation, and they are basically as follows:

a. *maxims of quantity*—make your conversational contribution as informative as required, viz., don't say too little and don't say too much.

b. *maxims of quality*—don't say what you believe to be false, and don't say something if you do not have adequate evidence for it.

c. *maxim of relevance*—make your contribution relevant to the conversation.

d. *maxims of manner*—avoid obscurity, ambiguity, be brief and orderly.[2]

As noted, these maxims apply to ordinary conversations. In other speech situations, some of these maxims may not apply and others might be followed instead. (The maxims of quality, for instance, are often not quite expected to be followed in political speeches.) The maxims of conversation are not, generally, conventions. The maxims are norms that directly instantiate the specific functions or purposes of communicative interactions and facilitate those functions. Some specific conventional settings, however, may determine what kind of maxims are relevant and should be followed. It is part of the conventions of theater, for instance, that some of the regular conversational maxims are suspended, and this is something that follows from the conventions constituting theater. Barring such unusual contexts, however, conversational maxims are not conventions.[3]

---

[2] Grice, *Studies in the Ways of Words*, 28.

[3] There are some interesting cultural variations with respect to the maxims of quality. In some cultures the general expectation of truthfulness, even in regular conversational contexts, is somewhat more relaxed than in other cultures. It is tempting to see this as a matter of social conventions, but I doubt it that a conventional explanation would capture the truth here. Not every cultural difference of this kind is necessarily conventional.

The next step is introduced by the notion of implicatures. A certain content is implicated by a speaker if it is not part of what the speaker said (viz., it is not part of the semantic content of the sentence uttered in the context of its utterance), but nevertheless implicated by what the speaker said in the specific speech situation, given the conversational maxims that apply. In other words, a speaker S conversationally implicates q by saying p in context C, if and only if

a. S observes the relevant conversational maxims in C,
b. the assumption that S meant (or intended that) q is required in order to make sense of S's utterance of p in context C, given the conversational maxims that apply,
c. S believes/assumes that his/her hearers can recognize condition b, and can recognize that S knows that.[4]

To mention one familiar example, consider the following situation: X, standing near his immobilized car that ran out of gas, asks for the help a local person, Y. Knowing these facts, Y says, "There is a gas station in the next village." Now, Y has not actually *said* that the gas station is open and will have gas to sell. But given the maxims of conversation (e.g., be relevant, don't say something you believe to be false), it would be natural to assume that these were implicated by what Y has said.[5]

The main question I would like to raise here is whether there are cases in which implicatures are determined by conventions. In other words, are there cases in which saying p in context of type C *conventionally implicates*, but does not say, that q. Grice apparently thought that there are such cases. At several points he alludes to the idea that there are *conventional implicatures*,[6] but explains them nowhere. It is a well-known puzzle in the literature on Grice that it is very difficult to surmise what Grice thought that conventional implicatures are. Interestingly, how-

---

[4] This last condition of transparency is actually rather problematic and controversial. Grice himself was aware of a serious problem here considering the implicatures involved in using disjunction. See *Studies in the Way of Words*, 49, and Soames, "Drawing the Line."

[5] *Studies in the Way of Words*, 32.

[6] Ibid., 24–26, 41, 46, 86.

ever, at one point Grice actually suggested a subtle distinction between two types of such cases: "generalized conversational implicatures" and "conventional implicatures."[7] Let's take a look at his examples.

As examples of *generalized conversational implicatures* Grice gives the following:

> Anyone who uses a sentence of the form X *is meeting a woman this evening* would normally implicate that the person to be met was someone other than X's wife, mother, sister or perhaps even close Platonic friend. Similarly, if I were to say X *went into a house yesterday and found a tortoise inside the front door*, my hearer would normally be surprised if some time later I revealed the house was X's own.[8]

Now compare this to conventional implicatures; at the one point where Grice gives a sense of what he had in mind, he says:

> In some cases the conventional meaning of the words used will determine what is implicated, besides helping to determine what is said. If I say (smugly), *He is an Englishman; he is, therefore, brave*, I have certainly committed myself, by virtue of the meaning of my words, to its being the case that his being brave is a consequence of (follows from) his being an Englishman. But . . . I do not want to say that I have said (in the favored sense) that it follows from his being an Englishman that he is brave, though I have certainly indicated, and so implicated, that this is so.[9]

There is a lot in these two passages that is puzzling, not least, the alleged distinction between the two types of cases. Let's begin by taking a closer look at Grice's particular example of conventional implicature. "X is P, X is, therefore, Q"; does it not simply mean, semantically, that is, that X's being P is causally connected to X's being Q? Is it not what the word "therefore" means in English? Consider a very similar sentence: "X had a lot of work today; X is, therefore, very tired."

[7] Ibid., 37.
[8] Ibid.
[9] Ibid., 25.

It is, I think, mistaken to suggest that anything is implicated here, as opposed to just said. Perhaps we can improve the example by removing the word "therefore." Suppose someone says (smugly, if you like), "X is brave, he is an Englishman"; or, perhaps, "X is brave; after all, he is an Englishman." Now here, for sure, it is *not said* that being brave is a consequence of being an Englishman, but indeed, seems to be implicated by it. It would be surprising, or puzzling, if the speaker immediately added "and of course, Englishmen are cowards" or such. Now, whether this case is, indeed, a matter of conventions, remains to be seen. First, let's try to see how to distinguish such cases from the examples of *generalized conversational* implicatures, such as "X is meeting a woman this evening," implicating that the woman in question is not X's wife (or sister, or such).

Why is the latter conversationally implicated, and not conventionally? How is it dependent on specific utterance situations or contexts? Here is a clue: A speaker can say, "X is meeting a woman this evening" and immediately add "I wonder if the woman is X's wife or not." Here, the implicature is explicitly canceled by the latter sentence. Now, what Grice seems to suggest is that in the noncanceled cases, so to speak, when somebody says "an X," failing to specify whose X it is, the expression would normally implicate that one has no specific knowledge about it or that one deems it irrelevant to the context to specify whose X it is. Otherwise, the speaker would simply fail to follow the conversational maxim of quantity (don't say too little). Similarly, when a speaker says, "I sat in a car for an hour last night," the speaker would implicate that it was not his own car. But again, such implication can be canceled by adding, say: "I had really too much to drink; perhaps I was sitting in my own car."

So here is the idea, I think: expressions containing "an X" normally implicate that the speaker has no specific knowledge about who's X it is, or about how X is related to somebody spoken about. That is so because otherwise the speaker would fail to follow the *conversational* maxim of quantity. However, such implications can be canceled on specific occasions; this should not be surprising since it is generally the nature of conversational implicatures that they can be canceled explicitly. (Recall our first example, "There is a gas station is in the next village"; the speaker can easily cancel the implication by adding "But it may not be open.") In other words, generalized conversational implicatures are created by a combination of the semantic features of certain standard expressions in natural language—hence the generality—and particular contexts in which the conversational maxims apply. Expressions of the form "an X" are semantically such that they generate a certain type of expectation; given the conversational maxims that apply in concrete speech situations, this expectation normally generates an implicature.

This may give us a clue to the distinction between generalized conversational implicatures and conventional implicatures. If it is, indeed, the case that sometimes the "conventional meaning of the words used will determine what is implicated," then those would be cases in which the implicature is not cancelable by the speaker.[10] Again, compare these two pairs of sentences:

1a. "X is seeing a woman this evening" *and*
 b. "I wonder if the woman is X's wife"
2 a. "X is an Englishman, he is [therefore] brave"*and*
 b. "Englishmen are cowards"

Clearly enough, pair (1) makes perfect sense, whereas pair (2) is perplexing; it just makes no sense. There is a general lesson here. According to Grice, there are two main features that must be present for an implicature to be conversational. First, as we have just seen, conversational implicatures are always cancelable. Conventional implicatures are not. Second, and not least important, Grice has emphasized that in order to determine that something has been conversationally implicated, one must go through a process of *derivation*, producing "an account of how it could have arisen and why it is there."[11] Both of these features, of course, derive from the fact that conversational implicatures are context-dependent.

Now we can generalize the puzzle about conventional implicatures: if q is *conventionally* implicated by uttering p—and

---

[10] That is, barring some very unusual circumstances.
[11] Grice, "Presupposition and Conversational Implicature," 187.

thus not cancelable—why is it not part of the semantic content, or meaning, of p that q? Before we proceed, let's remove one possible reply from the table. As Grice himself acknowledges, it often happens that some specific conversational implicature becomes so commonly used that it becomes conventional. Consider these well-known examples: "Do you have the time?" or "Can you pass me the salt?" These are cases where what is said is, literally, a question (about possession in the first case, about a capability in the second), but in fact, what is implicated is that you request the hearer to provide you some information or to pass you the salt. Now these implicatures are so commonly used that it is safe to assume that the expression has become an idiom. "Do you have the time?" just standardly means "Please tell me what the time is"; it is no longer an implicature. In other words, something that begins its life as a conversational implicature can end up becoming an idiomatic expression that has a conventional literal meaning that differs, somewhat, from the literal meaning of the words uttered.[12] Clearly, however, as his example attests, these are not the kind of cases Grice had in mind referring to conventional implicatures.

Let's get back on track. Presumably, the basic idea is that there are expressions in a natural language that by their meaning alone imply a certain content. Thus, consider the following examples:

1. "X is A *but* B"—implicating that the conjunction of X being both A and B is somehow surprising or particularly interesting.
2. "*Even* X can A"—implicating that (i) there are others, besides X, that can A, and that (ii) among the relevant agents, X is among the least likely to A.
3. "X *quit* A-ing"—implicating that X had done A in the past with some regularity.
4. "X *moved* from New York to Los Angeles last spring"—implicating that X had lived in New York for some time.

---

[12] This has been noted before; see, e.g., Bach and Harnish, *Communication and Speech Acts*, 173; Searle refers to these cases as conventionally used indirect speech acts; see his *Expression and Meaning*, 36–43.

5. "X *managed* to find A"—implicating that finding A involved (or, was expected to involve) some effort or difficulty.

All these cases exemplify one and the same phenomenon, namely, that a certain content is implicated as an integral part of the *literal meaning* of the words used (in the sentence uttered). Furthermore, note that none of the two conditions Grice attaches to conversational implicatures apply here: the implications in (1)–(5) are not cancelable by the speaker and there is no need for any derivation, for any story to be told about the specific context of the conversation, as it were, about how we got here. The implied content simply forms part of what the relevant words literally mean; it is *semantically encoded* in the literal meaning of the relevant expression.[13]

As a word of caution, however, note that the semantically encoded implication does not necessarily follow from the meaning of individual words; in some cases, different content is implicated by the same word used in different types of sentences. As an example compare these two sentences:

6. "Joseph was in the room, *too*."
7. "If Joseph goes to the meeting, the department chair will be there *too*."

In both cases, there is some content that is clearly implicated by the use of the word "too," but the content in (6) is different from that in (7): the implication of the use of "too" in (6) is that there are others, beside Joseph, who were in the room; the use of "too" in (7) implicates that Joseph is not the department chair.[14] Admittedly, these are very difficult cases, and it is not clear that they can be generalized to all anaphoric uses of "too." I only wanted to point out the possibility that the same word

[13] Note that the relevant implication remains even if the expression is embedded; for example, the statements—"It is not true that x quit A-ing," or "X did not quit A-ing"; or in the conditional, 'If X quit A-ing, he would be better off"—carry the same implication as "X quit A-ing," namely, that X has done A in the past with some regularity.

[14] This example—though not quite the point of it— is taken from an unpublished transcript of a lecture by Saul Kripke, "Presupposition and Anaphora."

might implicate a different type of content, depending on the type of sentence uttered.

Note, however, that in all these cases, the implied content, though semantically encoded, does not form part of what has been explicitly asserted. It is a commitment, and one that necessarily follows from the words used, but not explicitly part of what has been asserted. The relevant content here is only implicated, and not quite asserted, mostly because the implied content is unspecified. Suppose S says, "X is a politician but he is quite honest." The use of "but" clearly implies that S believes/assumes that politicians are not generally very honest people, or that it is somehow surprising—or perhaps just would be surprising to his hearers—that a politician is honest, or something along those lines. However, S did not quite assert this. Nevertheless, some such content is clearly implicated: when we are confronted with an explicit denial of the implied content, we would feel a certain unease. Suppose we confront S with a request for clarification: "Are you saying that politicians are not usually honest people?" and then, in response, S says: "Oh, no, I did not say this." Well, true enough, S did not say this, but we would also feel that there is something disingenuous in S's denial; it just doesn't feel right.

It may be worth noting that content that is semantically implicated is sometimes very difficult to distinguish from presuppositions. A presupposition of an utterance is the kind of content such that one can reasonably infer from the utterance either that the speaker has taken it for granted that her hearer already shares it, or else that the hearer would be willing to accommodate it as part of his background knowledge.[15] Now, mostly, this is a pragmatic issue.[16] However, in some cases, presuppositions look very much like semantically encoded implications. Consider, for example, the utterance "Bill regrets lying to his parents." The presupposition here, that Bill lied to his parents, or at least that Bill believes that he lied to his parents,

---

[15] See, for example, Soames, "Presupposition," 573.
[16] The pragmatic interpretation of presuppositions was introduced by Stalnaker, "Presuppositions"; see also Soames, "Presupposition."

would seem to be the kind of content that is semantically encoded in the meaning of the word "regrets." X can only regret that A if and only if X believes that A had happened. This is part of what the word "regret" means. This is not necessarily a problem, however. Presumably, a certain content can be both semantically implicated and presupposed by the relevant utterance. Not every utterance presupposition, however, is semantically encoded. As an example of the latter, consider this: "The Republicans and Senator Joe voted for the bill"; the presupposition here is that senator Joe is not a Republican. This presupposition is not semantically encoded, it depends on the conversational maxim of quantity.

Some writers have suggested that the semantically encoded implications are the conventional implicatures that we are after.[17] True, such implicatures are not cancelable, they admit, but this is precisely what one should expect, since the implicated content derives from the literal meaning of the relevant words or expressions. So it seems that if there are conventional implicatures, these would be plausible examples. It would seem that we have found cases where by uttering p it is conventionally implicated, but not quite said, that q. But is the implication here really *a matter of convention*? I would like to raise some doubts about this. The question is not, of course, whether it is better to call these cases semantic implications (as I would suggest) or conventional implicatures; there is no point in arguing about labels. The question is whether the cases under consideration are really conventional in the appropriate sense of conventionality that we have considered throughout this book.

Now, of course, if you think that the literal meaning of words is a matter of convention, you would be justified in assuming that these are cases of *conventional* implicatures. But in the previous chapter we have already disproved this line of thought. In other words, conventional implicatures turn out to be no

[17] Karttunen and Peters, "Conventional Implicature." Stephen Neale also suggests that these are exactly the kind of cases Grice has had in mind as cases of conventional implicatures. See his "Context and Communication," n. 20.

more and no less conventional than literal meaning is, in general. And since we have seen that the basic literal meaning of words is not, generally, a matter of convention, the so-called conventional implicatures are not conventional either. In other words, the kind of implicatures discussed here cannot be conventional since they do not admit of an alternative implication, as it were, that would have retained the literal meaning of the expressions used. If there is a language or an idiolect in which, for example, the word "but" implicates something else, say, that the conjunction is just as one would have expected, then the natural conclusion would be that in this idiolect, the word simply has a different literal meaning. It is a different word. And the same applies to the other examples, like the meaning of "even," "quit," and so on.

You may suspect that there is not much at stake here. Perhaps what is at stake is not much, indeed, but at least it is this: we have not yet found a case where by saying p it is *conventionally* implicated, though not quite said, that q. The cases under consideration proved to be different: the standard or core meaning of certain words (like "even," "but," "quit," etc.) is such that in using them the speaker *inevitably* implicates a certain type of content. What makes these cases unique, perhaps, is the fact that the implied content is somewhat unspecified. But this is not really very unique. The literal meaning of many words is such that it leaves a great deal of relevant content unspecified. Generally speaking, the semantic aspects of language both enable and *constrain* what speakers can assert, but they rarely determine the content of communication. Sometimes it may be clear enough from the conversational background what this content is, or it may not matter for the relevant conversation. Semantically implied content, I suggest, is not really a matter of convention. It follows, straightforwardly, from the literal meaning of the words used.

Christopher Potts, a linguist, suggested in his recent book that conventional implicatures reside in a very different kind of cases than the ones we've been looking at.[18] His main examples

----

[18] *Logic of Conventional Implicatures.*

of conventional implicatures are parentheticals and appositives. The following are two of his examples:[19]

   a. Ames was, *as the press reported*, a successful spy.
   b. Ames, *the former spy*, is now behind bars.

The italicized part of these sentences, Potts claims, are examples of conventional implicature. They are conventional because the implicated content stems from the "conventional meaning of words" used in the utterance. And they are implicatures, Potts claims, because they are "logically and compositionally independent of what is said."[20] From a semantic perspective, however, this is puzzling. To be sure, I don't want to challenge Potts's thesis that there is linguistically something unique and important about such appositives and parentheticals. But the suggestion that they are examples of implicatures I find problematic. Consider the logic of sentences of the form "X, the P, is Q"; or, "X, who is P, is Q." Logically, these are conjunctions. They both share a semantic commitment to "X is P and X is Q." In other words, somebody who says "X, the P, is Q" is logically committed to have said that X is both P and Q. If it turns out that X is not P, the conjunction is false. If I say, 'Hilary Clinton, the philosopher, is running for president," and it turns out that Hilary Clinton is not a philosopher, then I have said something false (though I may have also said something true; that partly depends on whether I have succeeded in referring to the relevant person, and this is basically a pragmatic issue; it depends on contextual knowledge that speakers and hearers share in the specific context of speech). Furthermore, the appositive is not cancelable. "X, the P, is Q" cannot be juxtaposed with "X is not P," or "I'm not sure that X is actually P," or such. In other words, the relevant content of such expressions is completely determined by what has been said.

   You might think that I have missed a subtlety here. Compare the following two sentences: (1) X, the Q, is P. (2) X is Q and X is P (or, X is P and Q). Though these two sentences are logically

---

[19] Ibid., 13.
[20] Ibid., 11.

equivalent, one is inclined to see the difference. It seems to reside in the fact that the speaker's commitment to X being Q is
more independent of his commitment to X being P in (1) than
in (2). But I doubt it that this can be generalized. Consider the
sentence "Scott, the philosopher, just published a new book."
The appositive 'the philosopher' may serve different conversational purposes, depending on the context of the conversation.
In one context, it may serve to identify the reference of the
proper name. Since I have two colleagues named Scott, one a
lawyer and one a philosopher, I may use "the philosopher" to
indicate which one I'm talking about. Alternatively, perhaps my
hearer has no clear idea of who Scott is, and by indicating that
he is a philosopher, I help specifying the content of my information to the hearer. And there may be other, different uses in
play. The crucial point to see, however, is that the implication
in such cases, if there is one, is purely conversational, that is,
specific to the context of the utterance. In other words, when
the utterance of sentences like (1) goes beyond what has been
said, that is, beyond the standard conjunction like (2), it does
so in virtue of the conversational maxims that apply and the
specific context of the conversation. The implicature, if there
is one, is conversational; conventionally, (1) and (2) carry the
same content.

To sum up: I tried to show that between semantically implied
content and conversational implicatures (generalized or specific) there is no space for conventional implicatures. I believe
that this view has the advantage of keeping the idea of implicatures context specific, essentially cancelable, and, generally, a
pragmatic aspect of communication. Implicatures can become
conventional, but in that case, they are no longer implicatures.
They become idiomatic expressions, acquiring specific literal
meaning in a general context of utterance.

CONVENTIONS IN SPEECH ACTS

The cooperative exchange of information is only one familiar
use of language. As J. L. Austin noticed a long time ago, there

are all sorts of other things we can do with words.[21] We can make requests, ask questions, give orders, make a promise, and so on. How language is used to perform actions (in addition to making statements) is the subject matter of speech act theories. There are many types of speech acts, and a great deal has been written about them in both linguistics and philosophy. We will focus here on one central case, namely, of performative utterances, when the expression of some words is, in itself, the performance of a certain action, that is, beyond the action of making a statement or uttering a proposition.[22]

In the course of the last few decades, two rival theories about performatives have evolved. On the one side, we find Austin himself and John Searle,[23] arguing that the performative aspect of language use is made possible by conventions. The utterance of certain words or expressions counts as the performance of an act of a particular sort only because there are certain rules or conventions that confer this performative aspect on the expression used. The initial plausibility of this conventional account derives from many examples where it can be seen quite clearly that the performative aspect of an utterance is conventionally (or institutionally) determined. Consider, for instance, the utterance "Guilty" made by the foreman of a jury; "Out" uttered by an umpire in cricket, or "The meeting is adjourned" uttered by the committee chairman. Other, less institutional cases may be such as introducing someone in a party by saying, "This is Mr. Smith," or greeting someone by saying "Hi." In all these cases, the kind of speech *act* performed is determined, or constituted, by social conventions (in addition to the rules or conventions that determine the literal meaning of the words used).

---

[21] Austin, *How to Do things with Words.*

[22] It is a well- known problem in the literature that Austin's original definition of performative speech acts is flawed, since he failed to recognize that just about any speech is the performance of some action or other, including the action of making a statement. This makes it very difficult to come up with a precise pretheoretical definition of what performative speech acts are. I hope that the detailed discussion, and the examples used, will clarify the nature of the cases discussed here.

[23] Searle, *Speech Acts.*

How to do things w/ words

The first stab in this conventional account of performatives was presented in Strawson's critique of Austin.[24] Conventions, Strawson claimed, do not play an essential role in securing the performative aspect of language use. Examples of the kind mentioned above are exceptions. Most performative uses of expressions in language succeed not by conformity to convention, as there is none, but by successful recognition of the speaker's relevant intention. Consider, for example, someone intending to warn his friend by saying, "The ice over there is very thin." There are no conventions that constitute the significance of this speech act as a warning. What makes it an act of warning is the successful recognition by the hearer of the speaker's relevant intention. Thus, Strawson claimed, barring specific institutional or conventional contexts (as in the examples above), the performative aspect of language use is not conventionally determined.

The second stab in the conventional account came with Lemmon's demonstration that that there are cases in which a statement is rendered true just by uttering it in the appropriate circumstances.[25] A performative utterance like "I promise to φ" is a case in point. By saying "I promise to φ," in normal circumstances, the speaker has made a statement that is true, and it is true in virtue of the fact that it has been uttered. Now, inspired by these two general points, speech act theorists like Bach and Harnish argue that performatives are basically statements, and like all statements, they can be true or false.[26] Performatives statements are expressions of attitudes, and a performative succeeds as such when the hearer recognizes the attitude/intention expressed by the speaker. "On our account," they say, "a performative sentence when used performatively is used literally, directly to make a statement and indirectly to perform the further speech act of the type . . . named by the performative verb."[27] Naturally, they conclude that there is no

[24] Strawson, "Intention and Convention in Speech Acts."
[25] "On Sentences Verifiable by Their Use."
[26] Bach and Harnish, *Linguistic Communication and Speech Acts*, and their reply to Searle in "How Performatives Really Work."
[27] Ibid., 98.

need for conventions to account for the performative aspect of language use. Normally, the hearer just infers the performative aspect of the speech from the literal meaning of the words used and the relevant contextual background that together provide the relevant information on the speaker's communicative intentions. With Strawson, Bach and Harnish maintain that conventional performatives form an exception, not the rule.

The view advanced here will be the rather boring one, that the truth is somewhere in between these rival theories. More precisely, I will argue that the statement-theory of performatives is generally correct and withstands the criticism leveled against it by Searle; on the other hand, I will show that there is a certain class of performatives—in addition to the institutional cases mentioned above—that is better explained by Searle's conventionalist account.

Let us begin by noting some examples. Consider the following utterances, assuming they are expressed in standard circumstances, that is, when there is nothing unusual in the circumstance of the utterance.

1. I *promise* to be there at seven.
1a. Yes, I will be there at seven.
2. I *apologize* for breaking this.
2a. Oops, I didn't notice.
3. I *beg* you to lend me ten dollars.
3a. Please, please . . . lend me ten dollars.
4. The meeting is adjourned.
5. You are fired.

Now some basic taxonomy: The expressions in (1), (2), and (3) are *explicit* performatives.[28] By uttering these words in normal circumstances, the speaker has performed an action and one that is precisely of the kind that the (italicized) performative verb—"promise," "apologize," and "beg"—semantically encodes. Utterance of (1) is an act of promising, of (2) is an act of apologizing, and of (3) is an act of begging. However, as (1a), (2a), and (3a) indicate, respectively, these performatives

---

[28] The term was coined by Austin and is widely used.

can be expressed equally well without using the explicit performative verb. It is not difficult to imagine a conversational situation where by saying "I will be there at seven" the speaker has promised to be there at seven, just as if she said, "I promise to be there at seven." The use of the explicit performative verb is not essential to the performative utterance. Finally, you will notice that performatives like (4) and (5) are similar to explicit performatives but also somewhat different. They are explicit performatives in the sense that the action done is the one semantically encoded in the performative word: by saying that "the meeting is adjourned," you *adjourn* the meeting, and by saying, "You are fired," you *fire* the person. However, the success of the relevant act here depends on some institutional context in which the speech has been made, and on the institutional role of the speaker. Only the chairperson of an official meeting can adjourn it, and only the boss can fire the employee. Let us call these cases *institutional performatives*. Note that the question of whether in such cases the same performative can be executed without using the explicit performative formula is a quasi-juridical issue; it depends on the specific rules and conventions of the relevant institution. In most cases, however, institutions do not require explicit performative words to be used. If the chairman says, "Let's wrap it up now and continue tomorrow," in most institutions this would be just as good as saying "The meeting is adjourned."

As we will see shortly, there are other types of performatives, and they may be quite different. For now, however, notice that there are two interesting conditions that all these examples seem to meet. They all meet both of the following two conditions:

> *A.* The statement, S, is rendered true simply by uttering S in normal circumstances.
> *B.* By uttering S in normal circumstances the speaker performs a certain action beyond the action of saying or stating that S.

According to statement-theories of performatives, *A* is the basic feature and *B* is secondary. Performative utterances, according to this view, are first and foremost statements. What makes such statements unique is the fact that when such a statement is uttered in normal circumstances, it is rendered *true* in virtue of expressing it. And this is not surprising, since such statements express the speaker's attitude or commitment. When I say that "I promise to be there at seven," I have made a statement, namely, that I promise to be there at seven, and by saying this, the statement is rendered true—it is true that I promise to be there at seven. Now, Searle agrees that performatives are also statements that can be true, but he denies that this is their primary feature. In his article "How Performatives Work," Searle advances the following argument against this account. He claims that this account involves an "obvious mistake":

> The mistake is that the argument confuses *being committed to having an intention* with actually *having the intention*. If I characterize my utterance as a promise, I am committed to that utterance's having been made with the intention that it be a promise, but this is not enough to guarantee that it was actually made with that intention. . . .
>
> Such an assertion does indeed *commit* the speaker to the existence of the intention, but the commitment to having the intention doesn't guarantee the *actual presence* of the intention.[29]

If I understand Searle correctly, what he seems to be claiming here is that the first condition mentioned above doesn't quite explain, or fully account for, the second condition. In other words, Searle admits that in saying, "I promise . . ." the speaker is making a statement, and one that is, in a certain respect, true, but the statement is true in a sense that doesn't quite capture the kind of performative that has been made, namely, the actual making of a promise. Why is that? Because the utterance of "I promise . . ." does not guarantee that the speaker actually has the intention of making a promise. The speaker is committed to having that intention, but commitment is one thing and actually having the intention is another.

It seems to me that if there is an obvious mistake here, it resides in Searle's argument. The presence of the actual intention to promise, that Searle claims not be guaranteed, is completely

[29] Searle, "How Performatives Work," 546.

immaterial; it is simply irrelevant to the question of whether a
promise has been made. The utterance of "I promise . . ." in
normal circumstances, amounts to the act of promising only
because it is the *expression of a commitment*. This is what the
performative of promising amounts to. Whether the speaker
actually entertains the intention is beside the point. The essential feature that makes a certain utterance a promise is the expression of the commitment, not the truth about the speaker's
actual intention. In other words, there is a crucial difference
between "I intend to φ" and "I promise to φ." The former is not
a performative, nor does it meet the first condition.

Now, you may think that this is unique to promising; or you
may think that this view depends on one's normative conception of what promising amounts to. The problem is that the
same features are present in other, similar cases. In saying, "I
apologize for . . . ," one expresses a certain attitude, and just
like in promising, there is no guarantee that the relevant attitude is actually entertained by the speaker. But here, too, the
presence of the actual mental state is irrelevant. You apologize
by expressing the apology, and in this you have performed the
relevant speech act, regardless of your actual state of mind.
Whether a speech act of apology has been made is one thing,
and whether the apology was sincere is another. Similarly, as
we sadly know, whether a promise has been made, and whether
it was made sincerely, are separate issues.[30] The actual state of
mind of the speaker is simply irrelevant to the kind of speech
act performed. Hence Searle's objection fails.

Thus, the conventionalist account espoused by Searle faces
a serious difficulty.[31] If performatives like (1)–(3) are primarily

[30] I am not assuming here that an insincere promise is not binding. On the
contrary, in most cases, it is. But this of course is a moral issue, not a linguistic
one. The question addressed in the text is whether a speech act of promising
has been made or not.

[31] In fact, there is another difficulty in Searle's account that I will not consider in detail. Not every use of an explicit performative word or phrase is necessarily an instance of a performative speech act. An unambiguous performative
sentence can be used literally without being used performatively. For example,
imagine that I am just signing some contractual documents and someone is

statements, then there is no need for any specific conventional background to account for them. The success of a performative utterance is fully explicable by combining the literal meaning of the words used and the regular contextual-conversational factors that contribute to an understanding of what has been asserted. In other words, there seems to be nothing special about performatives, nothing that calls for some additional conventional practice to account for them. That is, of course, with the exception of *institutional performatives* that gain their specific performative significance within the relevant institutions that may, or may not, be conventional.

Searle rejects this conclusion. Even if performatives are statements, as he acknowledges that they are, Searle claims that this would not be sufficient to explain how performatives function. What we need to explain, he claims, is the difference between things we can do just by saying or declaring that we do them, and things we cannot do just by declaring that we do them. You cannot fry an egg by saying, "I hereby fry an egg," but you can make a promise by saying, "I hereby make a pledge to . . ." Now, the point Searle is making here is that the difference between those cases in which saying so is doing so, and those in which it is not, are not semantic. Perhaps God could fry an egg by saying, "I hereby fry an egg." We can't. But the difference resides in the constitution of the world and its causal chains, not in the use of language. Statements like (6) "I hereby declare you husband and wife," (7) "I hereby declare that I owe you one hundred dollars," and (8) "I hereby end all wars and hostility between human beings" are all of the same semantic kind; they have the same semantic features. The differences consist in the relevant facts about the world.

asking me what I am doing; in response I say, "I'm promising to . . . X." In saying that I'm promising, etc., I just describe what I'm doing, I do not make a promise. Still, the word "promising" is used quite literally here, and as Searle admits, we have no reason to assume that the word is ambiguous. As Bach and Harnish mention, 'This raises a puzzle of its own: on Searle's account, how can an unambiguous performative sentence be used literally and directly whether it is being used performatively or merely to make a statement?" ("How Performatives Really Work," 98).

It is an institutional fact that when a marriage officer declares (6) in the appropriate ceremony, her utterance amounts to an action of some type; and it is an (unfortunate) fact about the world that if she utters (8), it has no effect whatsoever. Thus, Searle concludes, there must be "human conventions, rules, and institutions that enable certain utterances to function to create the state of affairs represented in the propositional content of the utterance."[32] Only such social-institutional facts can explain the (contingent) difference between (6) and (7) on the one hand, and (8) on the other.

On first impression it may seem that Searle is confusing here the perlocutionary effect of a speech act with its performative aspect. How speech affects the world is one thing; what kind of speech act it is, is another. Consider this case of the charismatic professor and his disciples: imagine that, unknown to the professor, his students are so devoted that everything the professor says they take to be a reason for their action and as far as they can, they just go ahead and do it. "X is a very good book," the professor says, and off they go and read it. And so on. Now, clearly, the professor's expression "X is a very good book" is not a performative. It is a simple descriptive statement. The fact that it happens to have the effect of inducing his students to read the book does not make it an order or a suggestion or such. In other words, you cannot judge the nature of the speech act from its perlocutionary effect.

Perhaps there is no such confusion here. I am not sure. But then, Strawson's critique of Austin resurfaces and should be decisive in answering Searle's argument. Searle's insight just generalizes from some cases to all. It is true that often saying so makes it so in virtue of social conventions or institutions. But this does not have to be the case. You can issue a warning by making a statement—"The ice over there is very thin"—with that intention, and when the intention is recognized as such, the expression is understood as a warning; you make it a warning by saying so. No particular social facts, conventions, or institu-

---

[32] "How Performatives Work," 555; note that Searle focuses on explicit performatives, but this does not affect the point here.

tions are needed here. Or, to take another familiar example, consider an invitation: by saying to John. "You are invited to my dinner party on Friday" you performed the invitation, so to speak; you have made it the case that John is invited to your party. Once again, I don't see where conventions are lurking in the background here.[33]

Before we declare victory for the statement-theory of performatives, however, let's pause to ask whether the two conditions we mentioned may come apart. As a reminder, here are the two conditions again:

A. The statement, S, is rendered true simply by uttering S in normal circumstances.

B. By uttering S in normal circumstances the speaker performs a certain action beyond the action of saying or stating that S.

Mostly, I'm interested in the question of whether B obtains without A. Those cases in which the first condition obtains without the second are easy to come by, but they are not particularly interesting here. They would be utterances of the kind "This sentence is expressed in English"; "I am speaking"; "I am here now," and so on. These are the kind of sentences that are rendered true by uttering them, though they do not amount to a performative. No act, beyond the act of saying the sentence or making the statement, is being performed here.

The crucial question is, of course, whether there are cases in which condition B obtains but not condition A. I think that there are such cases and that they prove the limits of the statement-theory of performatives. Consider the following performatives:

9. Hi (or, Good morning)
10. Damn you!
11. Congratulations!
12. Thanks.

[33] Of course there may be some conventions about how to invite people for various social occasions; but this is not necessary. Even in the absence of such conventions, you can invite someone to your party, or whatever, just by saying that you do.

Under normal circumstances, by uttering the kind of expressions in (9)–(12), the speaker performs an act; greeting, cursing, congratulating, or thanking. When I say, "Hi John" or "Good morning John," I perform an act of greeting. When you hand me something and I respond by saying "Thanks," I have performed an act of thanking, and so forth. But in none of these cases would it make sense to claim that I have said something true (or false). These expressions are simply not truth-apt, and thus none of them are statements. The way such performatives work is like making a move in game. There is a social-conventional game of greeting, and the game determines when and how one should make a move. The speech act of greeting is a move in this social game. And the same considerations apply to thanking, congratulating, and so forth. There is a conventional social practice that requires or permits you to make certain kind of moves in the game, as it were, and by uttering such expressions you just make that move; and in making such a move, normally you do not make any statement. Furthermore, it is noteworthy that most of these cases are explicit or quasi-explicit performatives. Though there are various ways of expressing thanks, cursing, or greeting someone, there is only a limited range of expressions one can employ to make the appropriate move in these social games.

Bach and Harnish would probably reply that there isn't really anything special about such cases; like other performatives, they are expressions of attitudes. The problem is, however, that performatives like (9)–(12) are not statements at all and they do not really express anything. In other words, the statement-theory faces two difficulties with such cases. First, they are not truth-apt expressions and thus they are simply not statements. Therefore, condition *A* does not obtain here. In saying "Good morning" I do not state that this morning is good, and in saying "Damn you" I do not expresses a statement about anything. Second, these performatives do not necessarily serve the function of expressing an attitude, though sometimes they may do that as well. Of course, it would not necessarily be an objection to the statement-theory that an utterance normally used to express an attitude can be uttered by an individual speaker on some occasion, without actually expressing the relevant attitude. But the problem here is that these performatives do not *normally* express an attitude. Thanking, congratulating, and even cursing are moves one makes in a social-conventional game, regardless of the actual attitude or sentiment that such expressions may express. Of course it can be the case, for example, that in expressing congratulations for a colleague's promotion I also express an attitude, say, of pride or some satisfaction. But this is certainly not necessary.[34] The relevant move in the social game here is to communicate the congratulations. It is basically a kind of ritual, a conventional form of a social acknowledgment, very much like greeting or thanking. Thus, the conventional account of performatives seems much better suited to account for such cases.

It may be noteworthy that in most of the cases under consideration here we cannot separate the literal meaning of the words used from the kind of speech act one normally performs by uttering them. The literal meaning of expressions like "Hi," "Thanks," or "Congratulations" is very intimately linked to the speech act that you perform by uttering them in normal circumstances. The meaning of "Hi," "Thanks," and so forth, is constituted by the relevant social practice and the kind of move you make in the practice by uttering these expressions. As I have indicated in the previous chapter, such expressions are very similar to single-criterion words, in that their literal meaning is constituted and exhausted by the conventional move you make in uttering them under normal circumstances. So here we have another example of words whose literal meaning is basically conventional.

Let us take stock. We discussed three types of performatives: we can label them institutional, general, and conventional performatives, respectively.

(i). *Institutional performatives*: some expressions gain their performative aspect by the institution in which they serve the

---

[34] It is quite possible that such performatives have evolved, historically, from the need to express certain attitudes.

specific functions that they do. Those institutions may or may not be conventional. In any case, in such cases the rules or conventions of the relevant institution determine that by saying X you have done Y. Normally, these performatives are role-specific: the institutional rules also determine the institutional role of the relevant speaker whose utterance of X counts as Y.

(ii). *General performatives*: These are the kind of performatives best explained by the statement-theory. No institutional or conventional background is required in order to explain them. Under normal circumstances, the literal use of the words uttered amounts to a statement that is rendered true by uttering them—because they express the speaker's attitude or commitment—and it also amounts to an act of some type beyond the act of making the relevant statement. In such cases, the success of the performative utterance is secured by the literal meaning of the words used and the hearer's recognition of the speaker's intention in making the statement. In recognizing the speaker's communication intention we understand the kind of action performed.

(iii). *Conventional performatives*: unlike (i) & (ii), conventional performatives are not statements; the expression is not truth-apt. In uttering such performatives the speaker makes a move in a social-conventional game, so to speak, and it is this conventional game that confers on the expression the performative significance that it has.

Whether this list is exhaustive I am not sure. I believe that these three types of performatives are the central cases, but there may be others. In any case, the fact that performatives are of different kinds, some are conventional and others are not, should not be surprising. There is a great variety of performatives and there is no reason to believe that all of them must fit one basic pattern.

Chapter Six

The Morality of Conventions

MORAL norms are not, generally, arbitrary and compliance dependent in the sense we have discussed in previous chapters. The reasons to comply with basic moral rules or principles do not normally depend on the fact that it is the norm that happens to be followed in the relevant population. Morality presents itself as a serious constraint on practical deliberation just by itself, so to speak; it makes certain demands on us that are based on reasons. Moral rules or principles are generalized formulations of such reasons. There is, I will assume here, nothing conventional about the idea (or rule, or principle, however you want to formulate it) that murder, rape, and torture are morally wrong and ought to be avoided. At least the basic or fundamental moral requirements or principles are not conventions.[1] This I will simply assume here; it is not the purpose of this chapter to substantiate this claim. Instead, I want to consider some of

---

[1] This is not uncontroversial, of course. Gilbert Harman, for one, argues that morality is basically conventional (e.g., "Moral Relativism"). In any case, I do not intend to suggest here that moral truths are eternal, or even necessarily universal, that there are no contingent or culturally relative elements in morality. Far from it. Morality can depend on cultural and other contingent elements in various ways without being conventional. For example, morality can have certain epistemic constraints that are sensitive to cultural or other contingent elements; perhaps certain things can only be valuable if people are in a position to grasp their value, and whether they are in such a position is something that can vary with environmental or cultural circumstances. See, for example, Raz, "Moral Change and Social Relativism."

the possible roles conventions may play in the moral domain. There are three questions that I will try to answer: First, what is the moral significance of social conventions? What kind of moral reasons, if any, would people have for following various kinds of social conventions? Second, I will consider the question of whether social conventions, and particularly deep conventions, have any role to play in the formation of some of our moral concepts. Finally, we will look into the question of whether the idea of a moral convention would make any sense; are there any cases in which a moral norm is conventional? I think that we can answer these questions without presupposing any particular moral theory, substantive or meta-ethical.

Moral Reasons to Follow Conventions

Suppose that in a certain community, P, there is a social convention, R, requiring people to φ under circumstances C. Under what conditions would it be the case that the existence of R counts as a *moral reason* for members of P to φ in circumstances C? And what kind of moral reason would it be? In particular, can there be a moral obligation to follow a convention? To be sure, I am not assuming that the boundaries of the moral domain are very sharp (or particularly important, for that matter). Some reasons for action are clearly moral reasons, others are clearly not, and then there are borderline cases. In fact, as we shall see below, many social conventions fall into this borderline zone. For now, however, a rough, intuitive conception of what moral reasons are, should be quite sufficient. So let us begin with the question of obligation: can there be a moral obligation to follow a social convention? In order to answer this question we must revert to the distinction between coordination conventions and constitutive conventions. A moral obligation to follow a coordination convention, though not very common, is quite possible and easy to explain; the structure of reasons to follow constitutive conventions is more complicated.[2]

---

[2] I will also say something about reasons to follow deep convention in the next section.

Coordination conventions, as we have seen, evolve as normative solutions to large-scale, recurrent coordination problems. Coordination problems of various kinds are typically presented in the literature in terms of structures of subjective preferences of the relevant agents. This prevalent talk about preferences, however, is potentially misleading. We need to keep in mind that people sometimes have a reason to solve a coordination problem they face, regardless of their subjective preferences. In fact, the agents may have a moral obligation to solve a coordination problem that they face. The conventions of the road provide a good example. The kind of coordination problem such rules or conventions are there to solve is the kind of problem that ought to be solved as a matter of moral duty. Avoiding collisions and accidents that are very likely to occur without coordinated behavior on the roads is an objective we ought to seek and take measures to accomplish. Therefore, if a convention has emerged to solve such problems, there is a moral duty to comply with the convention.

Well, this is not so simple. It would be wrong to assume that whenever there is a moral duty to φ, and ψ is a means to achieving φ—perhaps even the best means to achieving φ—there is a moral duty to ψ. Duties do not automatically transfer, as it were, from ends to means. There is always a question of alternatives, and there may be all sorts of reasons to refrain from ψ regardless of its contribution to attaining φ.[3] Bearing these qualifications in mind, however, it is plausible to maintain that if there is a moral obligation to solve a recurrent large-scale coordination problem, and a convention evolved that would solve the problem if it is generally complied with, then—other things being equal—there is at least a *pro tanto* obligation to follow the convention. My point here is not to propose a general, substantive moral principle; it is only to show that under certain conditions, it makes perfect sense to maintain that there is a moral obligation to comply with a coordination convention.

Needless to say, most coordination conventions are not of this kind, and in two respects. First, the reasons to solve a coordination problem, even a large-scale recurrent coordination

---

[3] See, for example, Brunero, "Two Approaches."

problem, are not always particularly strong or compelling reasons. There are countless circumstances in which coordinated conduct would have been better than the lack of coordination. But in most cases, this is just a matter of convenience, rarely a matter of great importance. Second, the reasons to solve a coordination problem often have nothing to do with morality. (Note that this is a separate point; the coordination conventions of language are very important, but they are not morally important; from a moral perspective it might be perfectly okay not to speak at all.)

Finally, we should keep in mind that even in the case of a coordination convention that we ought to follow, we have a good reason to comply with the convention not simply because it is a convention, but because it is a convention that happens to solve a problem that we have good reasons to solve. As I have already noted in chapter 2, in the case of coordination conventions, the reasons for having the convention in the first place, and the reasons for complying with it on each particular occasion, are basically the same reasons. Therefore, generally speaking, the question of whether there are moral reasons to comply with a coordination convention simply depends on the kind of coordination problem that the convention is there to solve, and the kind of reasons that the relevant agents have for seeking a solution to that problem.

Constitutive conventions are different. Conventions that constitute social practices, as we noted, have a dual function: both constitutive and regulative. The norms function to constitute the relevant practice, and at the same time they also regulate behavior within the practice. Now, when you look at the regulative aspect of such norms, many of them may look like norms that impose an obligation: "under circumstances C, do φ" or "under circumstances C, you may not φ," and so on. The rules of chess, for example, can easily be formulated in terms of a set of such rules prescribing permissible and impermissible moves (e.g., "You may only move the bishop diagonally" or "You may only move the king one square at a time"). But it is easy to see that the normative aspect of such rules is entirely conditional on one's reasons or preferences to play this particular game. Such rules basically tell you that *if you want to play chess*, this is how it is done. This "if clause" is a necessary, albeit mostly implicit, prologue to each and every set of constitutive conventions. One's reason to comply with constitutive conventions is conditioned by the reasons to participate in the social practice constituted by the conventions.

The example of chess, however, is misleadingly too simple. The conventions determine what the game is, and they also determine permissible and impermissible moves in the game. But of course, these conventions only regulate the behavior of those who want to play chess. You may decide not to play for no reason at all, and this would be fine. And if you do decide to play the game, your particular reasons for playing chess are not very important—that is, as long as your reasons do not substantially conflict with the values that chess is taken to instantiate. Perhaps we need to be more precise here. As we saw in chapter 2, it is certainly possible for various participants in a conventional social practice to have different and even competing conceptions of the values the practice is there to instantiate. There is no need to assume that a conventional practice cannot flourish unless all of its participants share a unified conception of its point or values. But, roughly, they must share a certain minimal level of commitment to engage in the practice as it is constituted by its rules, and they must share some plausible conception of the point of the practice and its basic values. In other words, at least with respect to practices like the game of chess, the constitutive conventions provide reasons for action only for those who are committed participants in the practice. What makes you a committed participant seems to matter very little.

Not every conventional practice is like chess, however. And there are two related questions here: First, are there any cases in which we may have moral reasons, perhaps even a moral obligation, to play the game, as it were? Are there cases, in other words, where it would be morally wrong not to participate in a conventional social practice? Second, there is a related, difficult question here about participation in conventional practices that are not really voluntary. As we noted in chapter 2, some conventional practices, like chess, are such that we need to opt in to

them; others, however, are such that we find ourselves participants in them by default, so to speak, and at most the question
is whether we can opt out of them. And as we noted, opting out
is sometimes very costly, almost impossible. So the question is,
how does this involuntary participation affect the reasons for
complying with the conventions of the relevant social practice?

Let me take up these two questions in turn. There are numerous conventional practices that are very valuable. It is difficult
to imagine a flourishing culture without them. The various arts,
sports, and other cultural activities can only flourish within conventional practices that shape them. These conventional practices serve important cultural and social values. Nevertheless, it
is very difficult to think of an example where one's nonparticipa-
tion in such a conventional practice would be *morally* wrong. It
may be silly, philistine, perhaps even shameful, not to value, say,
theater or poetry, or such, but it is not morally wrong. Neither
the production nor the consumption of such cultural activities
is a matter of moral reasons or moral duties. Undoubtedly, part
of the explanation for this consists in the fact that these conventional practices have very little to do with morality. They instantiate other kinds of values. And perhaps part of the explanation
derives from the nature of such practices; typically, cultural conventional practices can only flourish if the participants, by and
large, willingly engage in the practice and share its values and
commitments. These practices are valuable only for those who
value them.[4] Now, it is very tempting to think that there *must*
be exceptions to this; there must be conventional practices that
it would be morally wrong not to participate in. Perhaps so, but
plausible examples are not easy to come by.

The one well-known example that could be given here comes
from a certain conception of the morality of promises. According to the so-called practice theory of promises,[5] the obligation
to keep a promise is a two-stage affair: First there is a conven-

---

[4] I have elaborated on this in greater detail in "Do We Wave a Right to
Common Goods?"

[5] Hume probably held such a view; see *A Treatise of Human Nature*, book III,
pt. 2, chap. 5. See also Rawls, *A Theory of Justice*, 344–50, and Anscombe,

tional practice of promising; then, there is a duty to support the practice or, at least, a duty not to exploit it. Thus, according to this view, the obligation that arises from making a promise is based on the combination of the fact that there is a conventional practice, a "promising game," so to speak, and on a moral judgment that one ought to participate in the practice and comply with its norms (or, again, that one ought not to exploit the practice, that is, free-ride on it).[6] Had this been a correct view about the nature of promises, it would have been a very good example of a social practice, constituted by conventions, that we have a moral obligation to participate in, and comply with its norms. The problem is that this view is incorrect, at least insofar as it maintains that a *conventional* practice of promising must be assumed in order to explicate the obligation to keep a promise. Let me be precise about what exactly I want to argue here. The practice theory of promises is basically at odds with the kind of view, famously articulated by Thomas Scanlon, that the moral wrong of breaking a promise, or of making a false/lying promise, is just an instance of a more general moral wrong, or family of wrongs, deriving from what we owe to others when we have led them to form some expectations about our future conduct.[7] Now, it is not my purpose here to adjudicate between these two opposing views on the nature of promises, though I am inclined to think that Scanlon's view, or something very close to it, is probably the correct one. My purpose here is to show that even if promises must be explicated by invoking some general practice of promising, such a practice cannot be assumed to be conventional. In other words, even if Scanlon is wrong, and there is some social practice of promising without which

---

"Rules, Rights and Promises." More recently, an interesting version of the practice theory was defended by Kolodny and Wallace, "Promises and Practices Revisited."

[6] I am not assuming that a duty to participate is morally equivalent to a duty not to free-ride; for the purposes of the discussion here, however, the distinction is not important.

[7] See Scanlon, "Promises and Practices," and chapter 7 of his *What We Owe to Each Other*. See, also, Raz, "Promises and Obligations," for a similar line of thought.

the obligation to keep a promise cannot be accounted for, the relevant practice cannot be a matter of conventions.

The main problem with the conventionalist conception of the practice theory is this: In order to maintain that there is some conventional social practice of promising, one would have to show that the conventional norms constituting the practice of promising could have had some *alternatives* that would have served the same functions that promising servers in our social interactions. The problem is that it is very difficult to imagine what such alternatives could be. Note that the point is not that promising is somehow necessary to human relations; that there is no population that could do without it. Perhaps there is. However, as we noted several times, the mere fact that a population can do without following a norm N, does not necessarily render N conventional. What would have to be shown is that there is a conceivable alternative norm, say N*, that if the relevant population followed instead, N* would have basically served for this population the same function or purpose as N does. Now, think about the function that promising serves in our lives. Basically, promising is a communicated undertaking of a commitment about one's future conduct. It serves our ability to generate expectations about our conduct in the future that others can rely on and adjust their conduct accordingly. Undoubtedly, this ability to undertake a commitment and our ability to coordinate our actions on the basis of such mutual commitments are essential aspects of human agency. What would be an alternative normative practice that could substitute promising for this purpose? What kind of social practice, that does not involve promising, could possibly serve basically the same functions that promising serves in our lives? Unless the practice theory of promising can provide an answer to this question, it is not entitled to assume that the practice of promising, if there is one, is conventional in its nature.[8]

Of course, we could have had different conventions about *how to make* a promise. It is not implausible to maintain that

---

[8] For a somewhat related point, see Gilbert, "Scanlon on Promissory Obligation," 86.

certain forms or rituals of *expressing* promises of various kinds are conventional.[9] But this is not the issue; the question is how could we have a genuine alternative to the norms of promising that would basically serve the same functions or purposes in our lives; and I just don't see what those alternatives could be

Let me add a diagnostic point here: the misconception about the conventionality of promises is one of those rare examples, I think, where a misconception in philosophy of language may have led the moral analysis astray. As we observed in the previous chapter, the conventional theory of performatives, advanced by Austin and Searle, maintained the view that performative speech acts are only made possible by conforming to conventions. The speech act of making a promise has become a standard example. The thesis was that by saying "I promise to φ" the speaker has performed an act of promising only because there is some convention in the background constituting the performative aspect of such expressions; a convention of the form "Saying X, in circumstances C, *counts as* action Y" (just like saying "I agree" in the appropriate circumstance of a marriage ceremony counts as getting married). It is very easy to see how this conventional theory of performatives inspires, or at least lends considerable support to, the conventional-practice theory of promising. Both assume that the making of a promise is like a move in a game, a conventional game of promising. And then, of course, it would naturally follow that the moral wrong of breaking a promise must reside in the violation of the rules of the game, a game we have moral obligation not to exploit. But we have already seen, in the previous chapter, that the statement-theory of performatives better explains such cases. Promising is not a conventional performative. There is simply no need to assume any conventional practice at the background in order to account for the performative aspect of promising (be it an explicit performative or not). In saying "I

---

[9] Indeed, in various trades there are still some conventional rituals that constitute the making of a binding promise. A well-known example is the diamonds industry, where the striking of a binding deal is expressed by saying "Mazal u'beracha," which in Yiddish means something like "Luck and Blessings."

promise to φ" the speaker makes a statement about his or her commitment to φ that is rendered true by expressing it. Under normal circumstances, the expression of this commitment induces the hearer to form an expectation about the future conduct of the speaker. Of course, this would not be sufficient to explain how promising differs from other types of expression of intention to act, or from other types of commitments. A full moral account of promising is much more complex; there are many nuances and subtleties that a moral theory of promising needs to work out. And again, it is possible that some reference to a social practice would have to form part of the story here. But this social practice, whatever it is, cannot be a matter of conventions.[10] And there is no need for conventions to account for the performative aspect of promising.

As you may recall, I did suggest in the last chapter that, though promising is not a conventional performative, there is a category of performatives that is conventional. Greeting, cursing, congratulating, and so on, were the examples given. So perhaps some of *these* would be conventional practices that we have a duty to participate in (not cursing, I presume)? Maybe. It is conceivable that greeting, for example, is the kind of conventional practice that it would be wrong to defy; unlike chess, which you can decide not to play for no reason at all (and that decision would be perfectly okay), greeting is a conventional practice that serves valuable purposes regardless of one's subjective preferences or desires. It is wrong not to greet an acquaintance when greeting would be conventionally called for in the appropriate circumstances. But what kind of wrong? To suggest that there is a moral obligation to participate in a conventional practice like greeting seems a bit overzealous. Greeting, like congratulating, thanking, and countless other social conven-

[10] Although Kolodny and Wallace say that the practice of promising is conventional, in fact the conventionality of the practice does not play any role in their argument. They argue that social practices must be invoked in order to explain the *disposition*, on part of the promisers, to act as they promise. Perhaps social norms must be invoked to explain such dispositions, but as we noted in chapter 1, not every social norm is necessarily conventional. And nothing in their argument against Scanlon requires the conventionality of the practice.

tions of this nature (e.g., bring a bottle of wine to the host of a dinner party) are conventions of civility. They fall somewhere in this borderline zone between ethics and politeness, courtesy, kindness, and such.[11] The main ethical element in conventions of civility resides in the value of expression of respect. Civility is, at least partly, a matter of showing respect for other people. Now, it is true that such expressions of respect would seem to be rather weak, precisely because they are conventional and thus often ritualistic, almost mechanical. However, as we shall note in the next section, such conventions are often surface conventions that instantiate deep conventions, and thus often more important than meets the eye. Generally, the reasons to participate in conventional practices of civility are of the kind that is, perhaps, not predominantly moral, but not devoid of moral significance either. It is somewhere in between. (I will discuss this further in the next section.)

This brings us to the second difficulty. Once again, unlike chess, which you can easily decide to play or not to play, many conventional practices are such that we find ourselves participants in them by default. Conventions of civility, for example, are precisely of this nature. Such conventional practices shape our social environment. Learning to follow these conventions forms part of our basic upbringing and education. And this is true about other types of conventions as well, such as conventions of language, of course, but also social conventions that constitute and shape social roles and institutions, neighborly relations, conventions of fashion, and such. In all these cases, opting in is not a relevant question. We are all born and raised as participants, so to speak, and the only relevant question is the possibility of opting out. However, as noted earlier, opting out is not costless; conventional practices are typically backed up by considerable social pressure to comply. Deviation from such conventional norms is often met with criticism, hostile reaction, or social condemnation.

---

[11] To be sure, I am not suggesting that all these conventions are good; some conventional practices of civility are morally problematic, solidifying social hierarchies and power relations. More on this below.

Now, you may think that I have just contradicted an earlier point. The normativity of constitutive conventions, I claimed, is essentially conditional. It always presupposes an if clause: *if* you want to play the game, as it were, the conventional norms tell you what the game is and how to play it. But now I say that there are many "games" that you have no choice but to play. So what is left of the conditional? Let me be more precise here. The moral issue is not about wishes or desires. It is about reasons. The reasons to comply with constitutive conventions, I have argued, are conditional reasons. They apply only to those who are committed participants in the relevant practice: one has a reason to comply with such conventions only if one has reasons to participate in the practice, and undertake its basic commitments, which are constituted by the conventions. Thus, the relevant question here is whether lack of choice about whether to participate or not necessarily undermines this conditional nature of the reasons for compliance.

One might be tempted to reply that there is always a choice. Even if opting out of a conventional practice is very costly, socially, psychologically, or otherwise, it is still an option. You can always decide not to play the game. This is probably true, but it doesn't get to the heart of the matter. Let us suppose that, practically speaking, there is no choice; how would it affect the reasons for complying with such conventions?

I think that the answer resides in the following thesis: the moral significance of a reason-based choice to φ does not necessarily require that the relevant alternative to φ-ing under the circumstances is actually possible for the agent.[12] This may sound paradoxical, but it isn't. Consider this example: Suppose

---

[12] The basic intuition here is well known from H. Frankfurt's work on freedom of action. (See his *The Importance of What We Care About*, chap. 1.) Unlike Frankfurt, however, I do not intend to make here any point about *freedom* of action (or freedom of choice, for that matter). In other words, even those who deny the conclusions Frankfurt draws from his analysis should be able to concede that the moral significance of a reason-based choice does not necessarily depend on the actual availability of the relevant alternative courses of action. Whether this entails anything about freedom is not a question that affects the discussion here.

THE MORALITY OF CONVENTIONS

that X faces an option to chose between actions φ and ψ, and let us assume that the choice is morally significant. Now suppose that *unknown* to X, option ψ is not a real possibility for him. Had X chosen ψ, he could not have possibly done it. But again, X doesn't know this. So he deliberates about the options and reaches a decision, based on reasons, to opt for φ. Surely we have no reason to deny here that X's decision to chose option φ is a reason-based decision, and morally significant as such. So let us change the example and assume that the practical impossibility of ψ is known to X. Would this necessarily undermine the reason-based decision to opt for φ and its moral significance? I don't think so. Suppose that I am faced with a serious offer to perform a certain criminal act. I decline the offer *because I decide* that it would be morally wrong. I also happen to know that I just could not have performed the criminal act, no matter how hard I tried. What difference does it make? I have made a reason-based decision to reject the offer not because I couldn't do it, but because I believe that it would have been wrong to do it. You may suspect, of course, that my decision was biased; perhaps it was tainted by realizing the futility of choosing an option that I couldn't possibly carry out. As a psychological matter, this may be true. But it doesn't have to be, and it doesn't necessarily undermine the moral significance of my choice.

True, whether such choices are equally praiseworthy to those in which the relevant alternative is feasible, is a pertinent question. But it is a question that pertains to aspects of personal virtue and moral character. Perhaps it is the case that the more tempting and feasible the bad alternatives you avoid, the more virtuous you are in making the correct choice. But we are not talking about virtues here; the issue under consideration is about reasons for action, not moral character. Generally speaking, individual choices can be based on adequate reasons even if the alternatives are not practically possible for the agent. Therefore, there is no contradiction between the conditional nature of reasons to follow constitutive conventions and the practical impossibility of avoiding them on some occasions.

None of this means that the practical difficulties of avoiding many conventional practices are morally insignificant. They are quite significant when the conventional practice is morally problematic. And many of them are. Conventional practices often entrench prejudices and social hierarchies that it would have been much better to discard or abolish.[13] The fact that it is practically difficult not to comply with such conventions or to change them is certainly a reason for concern. Some conventional practices may be such that there is a moral obligation not to follow their norms. Complying with our moral duties is not always easy. But in this, of course, there is nothing unique. Many aspects of our social lives, whether conventional or not, are such that we ought not to support them, even if this is socially or otherwise costly.

THE ROLE OF CONVENTIONS IN MORALITY

Morality, I have assumed, is not, by and large, conventional, and most social conventions do not seem to have serious moral aspects. Nevertheless, it seems rather unlikely that conventions have no role to play in the moral domain. After all, a very substantial part of our social lives is shaped by conventions, and a very substantial aspect of morality is to guide our conduct in the social domain. Surely there must be some intimate connections between these two types of norms. Therefore, I would like to explore two possibilities here: first, I would like to explore the role that deep and surface conventions play in the ways in which some our moral concepts, and perhaps even moral sensibilities, are shaped. Second, I would like to suggest the possibility that there are some *moral conventions*. Let me take up these two points in turn.

---

[13] Even linguistic conventions can be morally problematic in this respect. Hungarian, for example, is a very hierarchical language. It has quite a Byzantine grammar that is very sensitive to social hierarchies and power relations There are at least three or four grammatical forms in Hungarian that speakers are expected to use, depending on the relative social position of the addressee. I must admit that there is a certain beauty in this complex structure, but it is morally disturbing. It reinforces hierarchical relations between people that should have been abolished a long time ago.

Conventions and Partially Descriptive Moral Concepts

Moral cognitivists and noncognitivists have long argued about the appropriate analysis of "thick" moral concepts. I do not wish to take sides in this debate, but I would like to exploit a simple observation that partly motivates it, namely, the fact that some of our moral-evaluative concepts are partially descriptive. Examples are familiar. Under normal circumstances, when somebody says "X's action was courageous," the speaker both commends X's action and partly describes it. By ascribing the predicate "courageous" to an action, one implies that it was done in face of some imminent danger and perhaps beyond the call of duty, or beyond people's normal reaction to such situations, or such. Similar considerations apply to numerous other concepts: There is a wide range of expressions in natural language that normally imply both a moral appraisal (positive or negative) and some description of the relevant conduct or character trait. One interesting aspect of such concepts (noticed by many philosophers) is the fact that their moral/ethical content and their descriptive content are inextricably linked. In grasping the meaning of such a word as, say, "courage," one would normally have to grasp both its evaluative and its descriptive implications. Even if I, personally, for example, tend to think that courage is typically stupid and not necessarily good, I would not have grasped the meaning of "courage" in English had I not known that it normally carries a positive moral appraisal. And *vice versa*, of course; one can only understand the moral appraisal that the word implies if one knows its descriptive content. (Imagine a speaker saying, without any irony involved: "Good for him! he was a courageous fellow, ran away from the bully just like everybody else." One would doubt that the speaker understands what the word "courageous" *means*.)

Needless to say, the fact that thick evaluative concepts are partially descriptive does not, by itself, render any aspect of them conventional. Conventions *might* play a role, however, in determining what counts as the satisfying conditions of the descriptive content of such evaluative concepts, and I think that they often do. Consider, for example, a concept like "rude." It is quite plausible to suggest that what counts as behavior that is considered rude is partly determined by certain conventions of civility. It may be rude, for example, to show up at fancy wedding ceremony wearing a swimsuit; or, worse, telling jokes during a funeral. As these example show, part of what rudeness consists in is precisely behavior that flouts certain conventions of civility. Had it been the convention that people come to weddings wearing swimsuits, such behavior would not be rude; and it is certainly possible to imagine a community that finds it easier to cope with grief by encouraging jocular behavior during funerals. And so on and so forth.

Now, you might think that "rude" is too easy an example because "rude" is a concept that, by its very meaning, implicitly refers to conventional behavior; it is just part of what "rude" means, namely, that one's behavior flouts certain conventions of civility. Perhaps, but other similar examples are abundant. Consider such partially descriptive concepts as "noble," "kind" (or "unkind"), "considerate" (or "inconsiderate"), "friendly," "charitable," and so on. Let us consider the idea of "kindness," which is probably the least obvious case. We appraise a conduct as "kind" when the conduct exhibits a particular concern for the well-being of another. But of course, not every conduct that exhibits concern for another's well-being is necessarily kind. By not humiliating you I may exhibit a concern for your well-being, but avoiding humiliation is not a manifestation of kindness. It is something we should all do as a matter of course. Kindness is a concern for another's well-being that goes beyond the normal requirements of caring for others under the circumstances. And now you can see where I am heading: to understand what kindness is (or to apply this concept correctly), one would first need to have grasped the normal background against which kindness stands out as a particular concern for others, and these conditions of normality are sometimes determined by the conventions that prevail in the relevant social circumstances. (Showing up with a bottle of wine for the hosts of the dinner party you attend is not kind if everybody is expected to bring something to the party. And thus, when the host says, "It's very kind of you," you both know that this is not the case, you're just complying with a prevailing social convention.) To be sure, I am not claiming here that all such conditions of normality are necessarily conventional; only that sometimes, and not infrequently, they are.

But now we can take another step. It is typically the case that the conventions that determine the background conditions of partially descriptive concepts, like "rude," "kind," and such, are surface conventions that themselves instantiate deep conventions. For example, it may be rude or inconsiderate (if it is) to show up for a formal event without the appropriate attire, say, for men wearing a suit and tie. Rudeness consists here, at least in part, in flouting a social convention. However, as we have seen in chapter 3, such conventions are surface conventions that instantiate deep conventions about ways in which people need to show some respect for others by their outward appearance. Similar considerations may apply, for instance, to the example of jocular behavior in a funeral. It would be very rude indeed, but only in the context of conventions that govern normal conduct on such occasions; these conventions, however, are probably surface conventions that instantiate deep conventions about ways in which grief is socially/publicly regulated, so to speak, in the particular community.

Again, I am trying to point here at something that is often the case, not always and not necessarily. Therefore, I don't think that an argument would be available to show that deep conventions underlie the background conditions of all the partially descriptive concepts we use in a natural language (or that they do that on every occasion). That is probably not the case anyway. I hope that the examples I mentioned here show that deep conventions may have such a role to play, and that the phenomenon is not esoteric or infrequent. More importantly, however, I think that the role of deep conventions would help us to get a better sense of the moral significance of such partially descriptive concepts. Deep conventions, as we noted in chapter 3, tend to reflect concerns that are deeply engrained in our social world and human nature. They serve relatively basic functions in our social lives. Therefore, by observing that the relevant conventional background we discussed here is itself an instantiation of deep conventions, we are in a better position to realize the moral-evaluative significance of the concepts that emerge against this conventional background. In other words, even if the conventions that tend to make certain partially descriptive concepts appropriate in the circumstances are not, by themselves, morally very significant, the fact that they are instantiations of deep conventions should help us to see that they are more significant, morally speaking, than one might have thought.

Now, I do not want to make too much of this, and for two reasons. First, because it is not the case that every violation of a surface convention is, *ipso facto*, a violation of the deep convention that it instantiates. As we observed in chapter 3, deep conventions are not followed directly; people follow deep conventions by following their corresponding surface conventions in the relevant circumstances. Thus, in complying with a surface convention, the agent also complies with the deep convention that underlies it. But when an agent violates a surface convention, it is not necessarily the case that he also violates the relevant deep convention; that depends on the agent's reasons for failing to comply with the surface convention. For example, if I show up to a formal event without wearing a tie, which is, let us assume, a violation of the relevant surface convention, it may be the case that I simply disapprove of, or just fail to observe, the tie-convention; whether I also disapprove of the deep convention that underlies it, say, the convention to show respect to others by some outward appearance, remains an open question. It is possible that I violate the surface convention because I fail to appreciate the significance of the deep convention that underlies it; or perhaps I object to the deep convention as well. There are various possibilities here, and it is difficult to generalize.

Second, and perhaps more importantly, we should keep in mind that the fact that a convention is deep does not render it morally or otherwise justified. Some conventions, even deep ones, may be quite problematic, even morally disturbing. Morality, as I have assumed all along, cannot be reduced to conventions. Conventions, by themselves, cannot determine whether a certain conduct is morally warranted or not. It all depends on the reasons for having the relevant convention in the first place.

Moral Conventions

Conventions are not, generally, moral norms. Nevertheless, I want to suggest that there are some conventions that are, in a sense, *moral conventions*. Roughly, the role of such conventions is to mediate between abstract moral ideals and their concrete realization in our social interactions. The idea that we sometimes need norms to perform such mediating roles is an old idea, that Thomas Aquinas called "*determinatio.*" When Aquinas considers the ways in which human law can derived from natural law, he says:

> [T]here are two ways in which anything may derive from natural law. . . . [The second is] as a determination of certain general features. . . . The second way is like to that of the arts in which some common form is determined to a particular instance: as, for example, when an architect, starting from a general idea of a house, then goes on to design the particular plan of this or that house.[14]

I take it that Aquinas's intuition here is pretty clear. How exactly it applies to our concerns here may be less clear. So let me present a structured argument. Consider the following possibility:

1. There is an aspect of our lives, call it V, that is morally valuable or good.
2. V is such that its realization requires certain forms of behavior on part of individuals in certain circumstances.
3. The precise content of (2) is *underdetermined* by (1).
4. Social conventions evolve that specify the kind of behavior required by (2) as instantiation of (1).
5. *Ergo*, conventions of (4) are moral conventions; they determine (in the Aquinas sense of "determine") ways of complying with moral reasons for action.

Needless to say, (3) is the crucial premise here. Let me try to clarify by giving some examples. Consider, for instance, the

---

[14] *Summa Theologica*, Art. 2, concl.

idea of charity. Charity is morally valuable; among other things it means that people who are at least reasonably well off should voluntarily give some of their resources to others who need them much more. But give to whom? And how much? How often? There are endless possibilities here. And, crucially, there is a wide range of possibilities that would instantiate the value of charity equally well. The ideal of charity is too abstract and indeterminate to specify particular norms of behavior that would instantiate it. We have a pretty good sense of what would be too little, or perhaps even too much, but it is impossible to say that the moral ideal of charity *requires* a particular set of actions in given sets of circumstances. In such cases, conventions may evolve that specify norms of behavior that instantiate the moral principle of charity.

I am aware of a certain difficulty about this example: Consequentialists may disagree.[15] According to a fairly standard consequentialist conception of morality, there is no issue of underdeterminacy here. At least in principle, we should always be in a position to know what is the correct action to perform: just how much, and what kind of, charity is required in any given set of circumstances. This means doing the right amount of the right kind of charity so as to maximize overall well-being (or some other conception of the good, as the case may be). I don't think that this is a plausible view about such cases, but I cannot expand on this complicated issue here. Instead, let me give some other examples that I hope will capture the relevant intuition. Thus, consider the idea of friendship. Friendship is intrinsically valuable; it is good in itself. And it is the kind of good that requires certain forms of conduct among friends. Some forms of behavior are expected of friends as instantiations of the values of friendship. But again, the value of friendship is too indeterminate to specify, in and of itself, what those forms of conduct necessarily are. Often a certain conduct is mandated as a direct

---

[15] The example of the indeterminacy of the moral principle of charity may well suggest that the kind of cases we discuss here are cases that Kant called "imperfect duties." This is probably correct, but I don't think that we need the Kantian framework to account for the idea presented in the text.

application of the value of friendship. But some of the specifications of what friendship requires are conventional. Different cultures have different conventions about friendship, conventions that partly determine how the value of friendships is to be instantiated in practice. For example, the level of intimacy that friendship involves tends to vary between cultures; or, in some cultures (Israel, for one) it is expected of friends to be particularly tolerant of spontaneity. In such cultures it is perfectly okay, for instance, to show up at a friend's door uninvited; in other cultures, such behavior would be rather unfriendly.[16]

Finally, consider the idea of respect. There are countless circumstances in our lives where it is morally appropriate to show respect to other people. These circumstances are very diverse, and quite possibly, not all of them instantiate the same moral conception of respect.[17] The point is, however, that showing respect to another person, that is, actually manifesting respect in the form of a certain outward or perceptible conduct, is often valuable and morally required. But again, such values are very vague, and we often need social conventions to specify the kind of conduct that would instantiate those values.[18]

Indeed, countless social conventions play this role of determining circumstances in which respect needs to be shown and the ways in which it has to be done. Some of the examples we discussed in the previous section are precisely of this kind. Conventions serve several functions here. First, manifestation of respect is often based on a symbolic gesture, and typically this symbolism is conferred on the action by the social convention that requires it. Second, the conventions determine the particular circumstances in which such conduct is called for. Third, the conventions specify the kind of conduct that is required in those circumstances, thus alleviating the need to deliberate in each and every case about how exactly one should behave.

---

[16] I am not suggesting that all these cultural variations are necessarily conventional. Plausibly, however, some of them are.

[17] See, for example, Darwall, "Two Kinds of Respect."

[18] On the idea of moral vagueness, see Shafer-Landau, "Vagueness, Borderline Cases and Moral Realism."

You may still wonder what makes such social conventions species of moral norms. Basically, the answer is that such conventions directly instantiate moral values and moral reasons for action. Their main function, we assumed, is to concretize (viz., "determine" in Aquinas's sense) conduct that is morally required. In this sense, they are moral norms. But they are also conventions, which means that they are arbitrary norms (in the technical sense we have discussed in the first chapters). The same moral values could have been instantiated by different social norms that would have served us just as well.

Two important caveats need to be mentioned. First, we must bear in mind that the evaluative conceptions instantiated by such conventions are not necessarily commendable. There are many conventional practices that determine or concretize socially prevailing ideals that are morally wrong, such as racism and gender discrimination.

Second, and quite apart from this obvious point, even in the case of genuinely positive moral conventions, the reasons for complying with them are typically weak reasons; and that is because the same abstract values that are concretized or instantiated by the convention can often be realized in other, equally successful, ways. Consider, for example, a convention instantiating charity. Suppose that in a certain community there is a convention to make an annual donation to the local church, say, of clothes for poor children. Now, there is a sense in which one's reason to comply with this convention is, indeed, a compliance-dependent reason. You make this particular annual donation partly because others in your community do it as well. And this makes perfect sense because the convention instantiates a commendable value; it is important to help poor children, and this donation is one way to do it. But in such cases, there are many other ways in which you can comply with the same abstract principle. Perhaps instead of the annual donation to the local church, you make your donation to another charitable foundation that helps poor children. Or perhaps you spend some time with the children helping them with their homework. The possibilities are numerous and not necessarily inferior to the conventional practice. I think that this case, though perhaps a bit too simple, is typical. Whenever conventions function to concretize abstract values, there are ways in which one can comply with the relevant value-requirement by nonconventional means. Perhaps it is not always as easy as in the case of charity. Conventions of friendship, for instance, might be somewhat more difficult to circumvent. Such conventions often generate expectations about conduct among friends, and it might be wrong to frustrate those expectation even if an alternative, nonconventional mode of conduct might serve the value of friendship just as well. But this doesn't change the general picture here. Typically, nonconventional conduct would do just as well.

The result of this argument might seem questionable. On the one hand, I suggested that there are certain social norms that are both moral and conventional. On the other hand, I claimed that it is typically the case that the reasons to comply with such moral conventions are relatively weak reasons. The problem is that we tend to think that moral reasons are typically serious constraints on practical deliberation. If certain conventions are moral norms, one could have expected that they would provide serious or weighty reasons for action. Furthermore, as we noted above, some of these moral conventions, like many conventions of civility, are instantiations of deep conventions that are responsive to serious moral reasons. So how can the reasons for following moral conventions be weak? The truth is, however, that there is nothing amiss here. What makes the reasons to follow moral conventions weak is not the moral aspect of the relevant norm but its conventional aspect. It is certainly true that the values of friendship, for example, may constrain our practical deliberation in some very serious ways. Reasons for action generated by requirements of friendship might be quite weighty reasons, occasionally outweighing serious countervailing considerations. The relative weakness of reasons to comply with moral conventions comes from a different source. It derives from the fact that the conventional conduct is only one way in which the relevant moral reasons—serious and important as they may be—can be complied with. There are, typically, alternative, nonconventional ways of achieving the same moral results. And this is not surprising, given the fact that the role of moral conventions is to render abstract values concrete. Concretization can be achieved in various ways, conventional conduct being only one of them.

Let me conclude by pulling some strands together. The two main parts of this chapter dealt with two different questions. Nevertheless, I think that there is a general lesson to draw from both. In their core or essence, conventional and moral aspects of our social lives are different in structure. By and large, morality is the direct application of reasons (and presumably, Reason) to practical circumstances. Conventional norms are indirect applications of reasons, mediated by patterns of general compliance that are contingent and path-dependent. Though most conventions have very little to do with morality, and most moral reasons do not depend on conventional practices, there is a certain overlap, or intersection, between these domains. In a range of cases, social conventions are morally significant. It is a significance that often derives from the moral significance of the deep conventions such norms tend to instantiate. Furthermore, as we have seen, some conventions determine moral principles, and in a sense, they are moral conventions. This intersection between the moral and the conventional, however, is rather tenuous. Moral reasons to follow conventions are very limited; and reasons for action created by moral conventions are typically weak, even if the relevant moral concerns are serious and important. Given the nature of conventionality we discussed all along, this should not be surprising.

CHAPTER SEVEN

The Conventional Foundations of Law

ONE of H.L.A. Hart's most lasting and influential contributions to legal philosophy consists in the thesis that in every developed legal system there are certain *rules of recognition* that determine what counts as law in that society. Such rules determine, to use a more recent term, the *sources of law*; they determine how law is created, modified, or abolished in the relevant legal order. In the existence of these rules of recognition Hart saw, as he put it, "the germ of the idea of legal validity."[1] The idea that there must be some norms that determine what counts as law in any given legal system did not originate with Hart. Hans Kelsen, one of the most influential legal positivists of the twentieth century, had argued that a legal order can only make sense if one presupposes its *basic norm*, the norm that grants validity to the entire system.[2] Hart's rules of recognition, however, are not presuppositions. They are social rules, and it is this social reality of the rules of recognition that is supposed to ground the idea, central to the legal positivist tradition in jurisprudence, that law has social foundations. As Leslie Green noted, however, a satisfactory account of these rules of recognition has proved surprisingly difficult.[3]

[1] *The Concept of Law*, 1st ed., 93.

[2] See, for example, Kelsen, *Pure Theory of Law*, and his *General Theory of Law and State*. For a detailed bibliographical note on Kelsen's writings in legal philosophy, see my entry on *Pure Theory of Law* in the *Stanford Encyclopedia of Philosophy*, http://plato.stanford.edu/entries/lawphil-theory/.

[3] See his "Positivism and Conventionalism," 35.

Why is that? To fully account for all the difficulties, one would need to tell a rather long story about the history of this idea, an account that I will not try to provide here. Suffice it to say that Hart's original formulation of the nature of the rules of recognition, as customary social rules that are "accepted" by the relevant population, rested on some general observations he had offered about the nature of social rules. These observations, which have been labeled "the practice theory of rules," turned out to be unsatisfactory, for various reasons that need not detain us here.[4] When David Lewis's theory of conventions came to be known, however, some legal philosophers have realized that in this highly sophisticated theory they can anchor Hart's insights about the rules of recognition.[5] Thus, a conventionalist account of the rules of recognition has emerged, and one that Hart himself, years later, seems to have endorsed in his postscript to *The Concept of Law*.[6]

Many contemporary philosophers of law, however, think that this conventionalist turn was a turn for the worse. Ronald Dworkin, for one, argues that there are no rules of recognition at all. Others, more sympathetic to Hart's legal positivist conception of law, argue that a conventionalist understanding of the rules of recognition is fraught with difficulties, and that such a view generates more problems than it solves.

Thus, the question I would like to address in this chapter is whether the conventional account of the rules of recognition is sound or not. I will argue that it is, with two important modifications: first, I will try to show that the rules of recognition are constitutive conventions, and not, as commentators generally

[4] I have elaborated on this theory and its difficulties in my *Positive Law and Objective Values*, 2–7.

[5] See, for example, Postema, "Coordination and Convention"; Gans, "The Normativity of Law"; Finnis, *Natural Law and Natural Rights*; and Lagerspetz, *The Opposite Mirrors*. J. Coleman has also espoused this view, though he no longer does. See his *The Practice of Principle*, 93–94.

[6] See the 2nd edition of *The Concept of Law* (1994), 256. Whether Hart's remarks in the postscript really amount to an endorsement of conventionalism is somewhat controversial. See, for example, Dickson, "Is the Rule of Recognition Really a Conventional Rule?"

assumed, coordination conventions. Second, I will try to show that the distinction between deep and surface conventions can be employed to solve some of the puzzles about the nature of the rules of recognition. With these two important modifications in mind, I believe that we will have the tools to respond to the objections that have been raised against the conventionalist account of the foundations of law.

The first step in the argument is to explain why we need a normative foundation to account for the idea of legal validity. The second step is to examine the nature of those norms, and see whether it makes sense to assume that they are social conventions. I will try to show that most of the difficulties with the conventionalist construal of the rules of recognition stem from the mistaken assumption that those rules are coordination conventions. Finally, I will present the idea that between the general reasons for having law in our societies, and the surface conventions of recognition that constitute what counts as law in a given legal system, there are some deep conventions of law.[7]

THE NORMATIVE FOUNDATION OF LEGAL VALIDITY

Consider the following sequence of propositions:

1. According to the law in a legal system S, (at time t), it is the law that N.[8]
2. (1) is true because N had been enacted (prior to t) by P.[9]

Now (2) clearly presupposes something like 3:

3. If P enacts a norm of type N in S, N is legally valid in S.
4. (3) is true in S because it is generally the case that X.

---

[7] I suggested the idea that there are some deep conventions of law in my "How Law Is Like Chess?" I now realize that there were some errors in that article that I hope to have corrected here.

[8] N stands here for a particular legal norm, of any kind.

[9] Assume that P stands here for any institution that is legally authorized to enact laws or legal regulations.

There is a logical sequence here: if there is a doubt about the truth of a statement of type (1), we would normally expect it to be resolved by an account of type (2).[10] And if there is a doubt about (2), we would expect it to be resolved by an account of type (3). And then we need an explanation of what generally makes (3) true, and so we get to (4). This much, I take it, is common ground. But now a question that needs to be answered is this: why is it the case that (4) has to be grounded in pointing to *norms*. Why could it not be something else?

Kelsen had a detailed answer to this question.[11] The law, Kelsen rightly observed, is first and foremost a system of norms. Norms are "ought" statements, prescribing certain modes of conduct. Unlike moral norms, however, Kelsen maintained that legal norms are created by acts of will. They are products of deliberate human action. For instance, some people gather in a hall, speak, raise their hands, count them, and promulgate a string of words. These are actions and events taking place at a specific time and space. To say that what we have described here is the *enactment of a law* is to *interpret* these actions and events by ascribing a normative significance to them. Kelsen, however, firmly believed in Hume's distinction between "is" and "ought," and in the impossibility of deriving "ought" conclusions from factual premises alone. Thus Kelsen believed that the law, which is comprised of norms or "ought" statements, cannot be reduced to those natural actions and events that give rise to it. The gathering, the speaking, and the raising of hands, in itself, is not the law; legal norms are essentially "ought" statements, and as such, they cannot be deduced from factual premises alone.

How is it possible, then, to ascribe an "ought" to those actions and events that purport to create legal norms? Kelsen's reply is enchantingly simple: we ascribe a legal ought to such

---

[10] Dworkin famously denies that this is the only type of answer to the question of what makes statements of type (1) true (see Dworkin, "The Model of Rules I," in his *Taking Rights Seriously*). But even Dworkin does not deny that a statement of type (2) can be, and often is, a perfectly adequate answer to the question of what makes (1) true.

[11] See note 2 above.

norm-creating acts by, ultimately, *presupposing* it. Because "ought" cannot be derived from "is," and legal norms are essentially "ought" statements, there must be some kind of an "ought" presupposition at the background, rendering the normativity of law intelligible.

Thus, an act can create law, Kelsen argues, if it is in accord with another, "higher" legal norm that authorizes its creation in that way. And the "higher" legal norm, in turn, is legally valid only if it has been created in accordance with yet another, even "higher" legal norm that authorizes its enactment. Ultimately, Kelsen argued, one must reach a point where the authorizing norm is no longer the product of an act of will, but is simply presupposed, and this is, what Kelsen called, the basic norm.[12]

According to Kelsen, then, it is necessarily the case that an explanation of type (4) must point to a *master norm* that makes it the case that certain acts of will create law and others don't. Without presupposing such a norm, the normativity of the entire legal order remains unexplained. But of course, the problem is that not much is explained by Kelsen's idea of a presupposition, either. Instead of telling us something about the foundations of the basic norm, Kelsen simply invites us to stop asking. In fact, the problem is even worse. As I have explained in more detail elsewhere, Kelsen's idea of the basic norm fails on its own terms. The idea that the basic norm is a kind of conceptual presupposition was meant to block a reduction of legal normativity to social facts. But in order to know *what* the basic norm in any particular legal system is, as Kelsen explicitly admits, one must look at the practice of various agents in that system, mostly judges and other officials, and observe what is the basic norm that they follow. The basic norms of, say, the U.S. legal system, and that of the United Kingdom, differ precisely because judges and other officials actually apply different criteria in determining what the laws

---

[12] More concretely, Kelsen maintained that in tracing back such a chain of validity, one would reach a point where a first historical constitution is the basic authorizing norm of the rest of the legal system, and the basic norm is the presupposition of the validity of that first constitution.

in their respective legal systems are. The *content* of the basic norm is entirely practice-dependent.[13]

This leads us to Hart's solution: Hart seems to have concurred with Kelsen that the idea of legal validity must reside in some normative framework, one that rests on some norms determining what counts as valid source of law in a given society. The relevant norm, however, is not a presupposition, as Kelsen would have it, but a social norm, a social rule that people (mostly judges and other officials) actually follow. This is what the rule of recognition is: the social rule that a community follows, the rule that grounds the answer to the question of what makes statements of type (3) true or false in that particular society.[14]

But now, if you take Kelsen's question seriously, you should be puzzled by this. How can a social fact—that people actually follow a certain rule and regard it as binding—be a relevant answer to Kelsen's question of what makes it the case that certain acts of will create the law and others don't? Crudely put, if you start with the question of how a set of "is" statements can generate an "ought" conclusion, you cannot expect an answer to it by pointing to another "is." Has Hart failed to see this? Not quite. Consider, yet again I'm afraid, the game of chess. The rules of the game prescribe, for instance, that the bishop can only be moved diagonally. Thus, when players move the bishop, they follow a rule. The rule, undoubtedly, prescribes an "ought"; it prescribes permissible and impermissible moves in the game. What is it, then, that determines this "ought" about rules of chess? Is it not simply the fact that this is how the game is played? The game is constituted by rules or conventions. Those rules are, in a clear sense, social rules that people follow in playing this particular game. The rules of chess, as we have seen, have a dual function: they constitute what the game is, and they prescribe norms that players ought to follow. Similarly, Hart has claimed, the rules of recognition define or constitute what law in a certain society is, and they prescribe (that

[13] See my "How Law Is Like Chess?"
[14] Hart, *The Concept of Law*, chap. 5.

is, authorize) modes of creating/modifying law in that society. Social rules can determine their ought, as it were, by being followed (viz., regarded as binding) by a certain community, just as the rules of chess determine their "ought" within the game that is actually followed by the relevant community.[15]

This cannot be so simple, however. The obvious difficulty with the chess analogy is that the rules of the game are "ought" statements, in the sense of giving reasons for action, only for those who actually decide to play this particular game. As we noted in the previous chapter, the normative aspect to the rules of chess is a *conditional* one: *if* you want to play *chess*, these are the rules that you ought to follow. But of course, you don't have to play at all, nor do you have to play this particular game. So it seems that by modifying Kelsen's account and replacing the presupposition of the basic norm with the idea of social rules, we have not made sufficient progress. The normativity of these social rules still remains unexplained. Hart was very much aware of this difficulty. He first tried to solve it by offering a general account of social rules, one that purported to explain the normativity of such rules by the idea of "acceptance"; acceptance is a complex attitude shared by the relevant participants that is manifest in their reliance on the rules as guiding their activities, as basis for criticizing those who deviate from them, and as grounds for exerting social pressure on others to comply. As I mentioned earlier, however, the main aspects of this "practice theory of rules" turned out to be very unsatisfactory. Hart himself seems to have conceded the difficulties, and years later, when he wrote the postscript to *The Concept of Law*, he seems to have endorsed the conventionalist account of the rules of recognition. As he put it, the rule of recognition "is in effect a form of judicial customary rule existing only if it is accepted and practiced in the law-identifying and law-applying operations of the courts." And in the following page he says: "certainly the rule of recognition is treated in my book as resting on a conventional form of judicial consensus."[16] Whether

---

[15] Ibid., 98–99.
[16] Hart, *The Concept of Law*, 2nd ed., postscript, 256–66.

this conventional understanding of the rule of recognition is an improvement or not, we need to examine carefully.

ARE THE RULES OF RECOGNITION CONVENTIONS?

Before we try to answer the question of this section, let me say a few words in response to a more fundamental objection to Hart's account, raised by Dworkin. He denies that the criteria employed by judges and other officials in determining what counts as law are rule governed, and thus he denies that there are any rules of recognition at all. But as far as I can see, Dworkin's argument is based on a single point, which is rather implausible. He argues that it cannot be the case that in identifying the law judges follow rules, because judges often disagree about the criteria of legality in their legal systems, so much so, that it makes no sense to suggest that there are any rules of recognition at all; or else, the rules become so abstract that it becomes pointless to insist that they are rules.[17]

The problem is this: To show that there are no rules of recognition, Dworkin would have had to show that the disagreements judges have about the criteria of legality in their jurisdiction are not just in the margins; that they go all the way down to the core. But this is just not plausible. Is there any judge in the United States who seriously doubts that acts of Congress make law? Or that the U.S. Constitution prevails over federal and state legislation? More importantly, as Hart himself mentioned in slightly different context,[18] there is an inherent limit to how much disagreement about criteria of legality it makes sense to

---

[17] *Law's Empire*, chap 1. The same idea is basically reiterated in his recent book, *Justice in Robes*, 164, 190–96. This should not be confused with a different, and much more interesting, claim that Dworkin also makes, namely, that even if there are rules of recognition, they do not settle the question of legal validity. Norms can be legally valid, Dworkin argues, even if they do not derive their validity from the rules of recognition. See Dworkin, "The Model of Rules I," in his *Taking Rights Seriously*. This is a large topic that I will not address in this chapter.

[18] *The Concept of Law*, 133.

attribute to judges, because the judges' own role as institutional players is constituted by those same rules that they allegedly disagree about. The role and authority of certain persons *qua* judges is determined by the rules of recognition. Before judges can come to disagree about any legal issue, they must first be able to see themselves as *institutional* players, playing, as it were, a fairly structured role in an elaborate practice. Judges can only see themselves as such on the basis of the rules and conventions that establish their role and authority as judges, namely, the rules of recognition. In short, pointing to the fact that judges often have certain disagreements about the content of the rules of recognition simply cannot prove that there are no such rules. On the contrary, we can only make sense of such disagreements on the basis of the assumption that there are rules of recognition that constitute, *inter alia*, the court system and the legal authority of judges.

So let us make the plausible assumption that there are some rules, mostly followed by judges and other legal officials, determining what counts as law in the relevant legal system. Are these rules conventions? Let us go through the motions here; in order to show that the rules of recognition of a given legal system, say R_R, are conventions, we would have to show that the following conditions obtain:

1. There is a group of people, a population, P, that normally follow R_R in circumstances C.
2. There is a set of reasons, call it A, for members of P to follow R_R in circumstances C.
3. There is at least one other potential set of rules, S_R, that if members of P had actually followed in circumstances C, then A would have been a sufficient reason for members of P to follow S_R instead of R_R in circumstances C, and at least partly because S_R is the set of rules generally followed instead of R_R.

   The rules R_R and S_R are such that it is impossible (or pointless) to comply with both of them concomitantly in circumstances C.

As we just saw, Dworkin's objection to the rules of recognition basically denies the truth of premise (1). But we also saw that this objections fails, so let us assume that (1) is true. Given the truth of (1), it would be extremely unlikely that (2) is false. If judges and other officials follow certain rules that determine what law is, surely they follow them for reasons. What those reasons, generally speaking are, however, turns out to be somewhat difficult to answer. In his original account of the rules of recognition, Hart suggested that the rationale of these rules consists in the need for certainty: In a developed legal system, Hart argued, people would need to be able *to identify* what types or norms are legally valid. In fact, he presented this advantage of the rules of recognition in providing certainty about the valid sources of law as the main distinguishing factor between "primitive," prelegal normative systems, and a developed legal order.[19] Later, in his postscript to *The Concept of Law*, Hart seems to have added another kind of reason for having rules of recognition, basically of a coordinative nature:

> Certainly the rule of recognition is treated in my book as resting on a conventional form of judicial custom. That it does so rest seems quite clear at least in English and American law for surely an English judge's reason for treating Parliament's legislation (or an American judge's reason for treating the Constitution) as a source of law having supremacy over other sources includes the fact that his judicial colleagues concur in this as their predecessors have done.[20]

I have some doubts about both of these explanations. That the rules of recognition contribute to our certainty about what counts as law in our society is surely true. But is it the main reason for having such rules? This I doubt. It is like suggesting that there are some rules or conventions about what constitutes opera so as to enable us to identify the operatic genre as distinguished from other, similar artistic performances. Surely, if there are some rules or conventions that constitute an operatic genre, it is because there are some artistic reasons for having this kind of genre in the first place. Similarly, I would suggest, if there

[19] Ibid., chap. 5.
[20] Hart, *The Concept of Law*, 2nd ed., postscript, 267.

are reasons to have rules of recognition, those reasons must be very intimately linked to the reasons for having law in the first place. Certainty about what the law is cannot be the main reason for having law. There must be some reasons for having law first, and then it might also be important to have a certain level of certainty about it. It cannot be the other way around. To be sure, I am not suggesting that the reasons for having rules of recognition are the same as the reasons for having law in a society. My claim is that the reasons for having rules of recognition are closely tied to the reasons for having law, and in some ways (yet to be specified), they instantiate those reasons.

The coordinative rationale of the rules of recognition is even more suspect, and for reasons that are quite explicit in Hart's own writings. It is true, of course, that judges and other legal agents, acting in their official capacities, need a great deal of coordination in various respects. In particular, they would need to follow basically those same rules that other officials in their legal system follow in identifying the relevant sources of law in their legal system. That the rules of recognition enable this basic kind of coordination in the various actions of legal officials is not disputable. But again, it makes little sense to suggest that this is the main rationale of the rules of recognition. As we mentioned above, for judges to have any coordination problem that might need a solution, first we must be able to identify them *as judges*; we first need a set of rules that constitute their specific institutional roles. In short, and more generally, first we need the institutions of law, then we may also have some coordination problems that may require a normative solution. The basic role of the rules of recognition is to constitute the relevant institutions. The fundamental rules of recognition of a legal system are constitutive rules (or conventions, as we shall see), and their coordination functions are secondary, at best.

I have to say that there is a rather striking confusion in some of the literature on the conventionality of the rules of recognition that connects these two points. Because the standard understanding of conventions has been the one offered by Lewis, which consists of the idea that conventions are normative solutions to coordination problems, commentators have been drawn to the idea that if the rules of recognition are conventions, their basic rationale must be a coordinative one. But commentators have also realized that the rationale of the rules of recognition must be closely tied to the reasons for having law in the first place. And the combination of these two points has led many to assume that the main rationale *of law itself*, the main reasons for having law in society, are also coordinative in nature.[21] This has rendered legal conventionalism, as this view came to be called, rather implausible. The idea that law's main functions in society can be reduced to solution of coordination problems is all too easy to refute. Solving coordination problems, as complex and intricate as they may be, is only one of the main functions of law in society, and probably not the most important one.

I mention this confusion here because Leslie Green's critique of legal conventionalism, often cited as a main argument against a conventionalist construal of the rules of recognition, is based on it. Green is absolutely right to claim that the authority of law, and its main moral-political rationale, cannot be explained in terms of law's function in solving coordination problems.[22] But he is wrong to conclude that this undermines a conventionalist account of the rules of recognition. Neither the main functions of law in society, nor the main rationale of the rules of recognition, has much to do with solving coordination problems.

We have yet to show, of course, that the rules of recognition are conventions. The conventionality of the rules of recognition crucially depends on the third condition, namely, on the question of whether the rules are arbitrary (and compliance dependent) in the requisite sense. So let us turn to examine this aspect of the rules of recognition. On the face of it, the arbitrariness of the rules of recognition is strongly supported by the following two observations: First, we know that different legal systems, even ones that are very similar in all other

---

[21] See, for example, Lagerspetz, *The Opposite Mirrors*, and den Hartogh, *Mutual Expectations*. Dworkin's interpretation of what he calls legal conventionalism, relies on a very similar idea. See his *Law's Empire*, chap. 7.

[22] See his "Positivism and Conventionalism," 43–49.

respects, have different rules or recognition. Second, there is very clear sense in which the reasons for following the rules of recognition are compliance-dependent in the relevant sense. This is one of the points that Hart has rightly emphasized in the postscript, namely, that the reasons judges and other officials have for following certain norms about the identification of the sources of law in their legal systems are closely tied to the fact that other officials follow those same norms.

Now, I don't think that either one of these observations that supports the conventionality of the rules of recognition is really controversial. The reasons critics have for doubting the conventionality of the rules of recognition pertain to the normative aspect of the rules. Again, Green was one of those who observed this difficulty in the conventional account of the rule of recognition. As he put it, "Hart's view that the fundamental rules [of recognition] are 'mere conventions' continues to sit uneasily with any notion of obligation," and thus, with the intuition that the rules of recognition point to the sources of law that "judges are legally bound to apply."[23] So the problem seems to be this: if the rules of recognition are *arbitrary* in the requisite sense, how can we explain the fact that they are supposed to obligate judges and other legal officials to follow them?

I think that by now we have all the tools we need to answer this question. First, even if Green had been right to assume that the main conventionalist rationale of the rules of recognition is basically a coordinative one, the puzzle he raises about their potential normativity is easily answered. As we saw in the previous chapter, some coordination problems are such that there is an obligation to solve them. If a conventional solution has emerged, the relevant agents may well have an obligation to follow the conventional solution. However, since I do not think that the rules of recognition are coordination conventions, I will not avail myself of this simple answer. The main answer to Green's puzzle resides in the distinction between the legal obligation to follow the rules of recognition, and the separate question about a moral obligation, if there is one, to follow those rules.

[23] Green, "Concept of Law Revisited," 1697.

The rules of recognition, like the rules of chess, determine what the practice is. They constitute the rules of the game, so to speak. Like other constitutive rules, they have a dual function: they both determine what constitutes the practice, and prescribe modes of conduct within it. The *legal* obligation to follow the rules of recognition is just like the chess players' obligation to, say, move the bishop diagonally. Both are prescribed by the rules of the game. What such rules cannot prescribe, however, is an "ought" about playing the game to begin with. As we noted in the previous chapter, the normativity of constitutive conventions is always conditional. Conventional practices create reasons for action only if the relevant agent has a reason to participate in the practice to begin with. And that is true of the law as well. If there is an "ought to play game," so to speak, then this ought cannot be expected to come from the rules of recognition. The obligation to play by the rules, that is, to follow the law, if there is one, must come from moral and political considerations. The reasons for obeying the law cannot be derived from the norms that determine what the law is.

Let me summarize and add a few observations. My main response to Green's worries about the normativity of the rules of recognition is this: once we realize that the rules of recognition are constitutive and not coordinative conventions, we can see that there is really nothing unique or particularly puzzling about the concept of legal normativity, or legal obligation. The sense in which a judge is obliged to follow the rules of recognition is exactly like the obligation of an umpire in a cricket game to follow the rules of cricket. Both obligations are basically conditional. If, and to the extent that, the judge, or the umpire, has reasons to play the game, they have reasons to play it by the rules, and the rules determine what their obligations in the game are. In both cases, however, we cannot expect the rules of the game to constitute the reason to play it. In other words, the internal (legal) obligation is determined by the rules themselves; the rules that constitute the game also prescribe modes of conduct within it. The external obligation to play the game, if there is one, is a different matter, one that cannot be expected to be determined on the basis of the normativity of the rules of the game. Whether judges, or anybody else, would have an obligation to play the game, as it were, is always a separate question, one that needs to be determined on moral-political grounds.

Now of course, all this assumes that the rules of recognition are indeed constitutive conventions, and not coordination conventions, as has been generally assumed. Therefore, let me complete the argument by noting some further, important difficulties with the idea that the rules of recognition are coordination conventions. Since old habits die hard, it may be worth adding a few nails to the coffin.

There are three main problems with the view that the rules of recognition are coordination conventions. First, this view misses the constitutive function of the rules of recognition; it misses the point that these conventions constitute, to a considerable extent, what law is. Second, the idea that the rules of recognition are coordination conventions is not easy to reconcile with the apparent political importance of these rules. Finally, the coordination conventions account blurs the distinction between the question of what law is, and what counts as law in a particular legal order. Let me explain these problems.

The rules of recognition determine how law in a particular legal system is created, modified, and abolished, thus also making it possible to identify what the law in the relevant community is. Notice that it is a rather complex function that the rules of recognition have; in determining the criteria of legality in a particular system, the rules basically constitute what counts as law in that system, and in this they also enable us to identify the legal domain as such. Very much like the constitutive rules of games, such rules determine what counts as the relevant type of activity. Hart's repeated reference to examples of games would clearly suggest that he himself was very much aware of this constitutive function of the rules of recognition. What critics seem to have missed is the fact that coordination conventions do not tend to have such a constitutive function. If there is a recurrent coordination problem and a social norm evolves to solve it, in this the rule has basically exhausted its function. Constitutive conventions, as we have seen in chapter 2, are much more complex. Conventions constitute a type of activity when they form a

whole system of interlocking norms, both constituting a social
practice and regulating certain activities within it. To be sure,
I do not want to deny that some of the functions served by the
rules of recognition are coordinative in nature. But the need to
coordinate the actions of various officials is only one aspect of
the rules of recognition. First we must recognize them *as legal
officials*, and this is only made possible by the constitutive function of the rules of recognition. Before any coordination problem between officials arises, we must know who counts as an
official, or a player in this game, if you like, and this is precisely
what the rules of recognition do; they constitute the rules of the
game and the various roles played in it.

And this brings me to the second point. Realizing that constitutive conventions tend to emerge as responses to complex
social and human needs, and not just coordination problems,
should make it much easier to understand why the specific
conventions we happen to have may matter to us, sometimes
a great deal. And the rules of recognition do matter, morally,
politically, and otherwise. After all, it does matter to us who
makes the law in our society, and how it is done. The rules
of recognition of legal systems are often politically important.
Consider, for example, one of the most fundamental rules of
recognition in the United States, namely, the rule that determines the supremacy of the U.S. Constitution. It should be
easy to recognize that this is no trivial matter; it is something
that most Americans feel strongly about, to say the least.[24]
There are political and moral values associated with rules of
recognition, values that it would be much less rational to attribute to rules that are there to solve a coordination problem.
There are, of course, many coordination problems that it is
very important to solve; but it is usually not very important
how exactly we solve them, as long as the solution is reasonably efficient.

---

[24] It is possible, of course, that people tend to project greater importance
onto the rules of recognition than is morally or politically warranted. However,
even if the precise content of these rules is less important than people tend to
presume, I think it is safe to maintain that they are not entirely mistaken.

Finally, the coordination account of the rules of recognition makes it very unclear how these conventions of recognition relate to the concept of law. Consider chess, again: without the conventions that constitute this game, there is no game of chess nor, consequently, a concept of chess. The rules of chess have a crucial constitutive role to play in constituting our concept of chess. On the other hand, if we think about a standard coordination convention, the picture is quite different: consider, for example, a convention that determines on which side of the road to drive, or how to spell a word correctly in English. In these cases we normally have the concept of the relevant activity irrespective of the conventions. In fact, this is typically so, since the whole point of coordination conventions is to solve a problem that had been there before the convention emerged, so it must be the case that we have a concept of the relevant activity irrespective of the conventions that have evolved to regulate it. Once again, it seems that law is more like chess than the coordination cases; without the social conventions that constitute ways of making law and recognizing it as such, it is difficult to imagine what kind of concept of law we could possibly have.

The Deep Conventions of Law

There are some reasons for having law, reasons that reflect the main functions of law in our society. For example, the reasons to have some authoritative rules of conduct, the need to resolve conflicts in society, to create public goods, to solve collective action problems, and so forth. And then there are, as we have seen, social conventions that determine what counts as law in a given community, namely, the rules of recognition. I want to argue that between the general reasons for having law, and the local conventions that determine what counts as law in particular legal system, there is an intermediary layer of *deep conventions*, conventions that constitute the main building blocks of the relevant legal system. The deep conventions of law are typically manifest in the surface conventions of recognition that are specific to any given society, or legal system.

A quick reminder of how deep conventions differ from surface conventions might be in place. As we have seen in chapter 3,

1. Deep conventions emerge as normative responses to basic social and psychological needs. They serve relatively basic functions in our social world.
2. Deep conventions typically enable a set of surface conventions to emerge, and many types of surface conventions are only made possible as instantiations of deep conventions.
3. Under normal circumstances, deep conventions are actually practiced by following their corresponding surface conventions.
4. Compared with surface conventions, deep conventions are typically much more durable and less amenable to change.
5. Surface conventions often get to be codified and thus replaced by institutional rules. Deep conventions typically resist codification (of this kind).

Let us now return to law. The thesis I want to suggest here it this: The rules of recognition, of the kind Hart had in mind, are surface conventions. They determine what counts as law in a particular legal system, in a particular community. These surface conventions of recognition are instantiations of deep conventions about what kind of legal system the relevant community has. There is a wide range of reasons for having law and legal institutions in our society. Law serves an array of functions in every society in which it exists. These functions constitute the basic reasons for having law in our societies. But these reasons, universal as they may be, can be instantiated by different sets of deep conventions.

What would be the deep conventions of law? For lawyers who are familiar with different types of legal systems, the answer would be very clear: over the centuries different types of legal systems have evolved in different parts of the world. Some of these types of legal system, like the common-law and the continental law traditions, are still with us, and in many respects, strikingly different from each other. Other, older traditions, like the feudal system, or the Roman law tradition, have ceased to exist. Now, what we call traditions, or sometimes families of legal systems, basically instantiate deep conventions of law. Let's take the paradigms of common law and continental law as our main example.[25] First, notice that the conventions that constitute each one of these traditions are not practiced by following the conventions constituting the tradition; deep conventions are practiced by following the surface conventions that instantiate them, namely, in this case, the rules of recognition of each particular legal system. In other words, American judges follow the rules of recognition of the U.S. legal system, English judges follow the rules of recognition of the U.K. system, and so forth, and not directly, as it were, the deep conventions of common law. Similarly, German and French judges follow the rules of recognition of their respective legal systems, not the general, deep conventions of the continental system.

Now, if you think about the differences between common law and continental law, reflecting, as they do, very different conceptions of organizing a legal order, you will immediately notice that though these two traditions are very different, they definitely respond to the same basic needs and functions that prevail in all the societies that have them. The basic needs to have law and a legal system, and the particular functions law has in these societies, are fundamentally the same. In other words, in spite of the considerable differences between the common-law and continental law traditions, the societies in which these systems exist are very similar. Law serves in common-law systems, like the United States, England, and Canada, basically the same functions that it serves in the continental systems like the ones in Germany, France, and Belgium. Nevertheless, the conventional solutions to the problems law is there to solve that have evolved in these two legal cultures, are rather different. I am not an expert in comparative law, and therefore I will not attempt to give an accurate summary of these differences, just note some of them. Common law, for example, assigns much greater role to judges in developing the law and adapting it to changing circumstances; continental law seeks to

---

[25] Other examples would be religious legal systems, like Jewish Law or Islamic Sharia, presumably, though I know very little about it, legal systems in Southeast Asia, etc.

restrict the role of judges in this respect, and allows them much less flexibility in changing the law. Legislation in the continental systems is very structured, typically seeking to codify entire areas of law in a very systematic way; common-law legislation is much less structured, typically avoiding codification of entire areas of law. In the procedural area, common law is committed to an adversarial system, whereby litigants argue their case in front of an impartial jury or judge; continental law is "inquisitory," not adversarial, allowing judges an investigatory role far beyond anything that would be acceptable in common law. And so on and so forth.

Let me summarize these points. In comparing the common-law and the continental law traditions, we can see the following: first, that they manifest very different forms of structuring a legal system. Second, that in spite of the considerable differences between them, the two traditions basically respond to the same needs and serve the same basic functions in their respective societies. Finally, the conventions that are actually being followed by judges and other legal officials are not the deep conventions of the respective legal traditions, but their manifestation in the surface conventions of recognition that are unique to the particular legal systems in play.

Admittedly, I have not yet shown that the underlying differences between these two legal traditions, the common law and continental law, are really differences in deep conventions. But what else could they be? The fact, well known and undeniable, that these two legal traditions have evolved as a result of various political events, and to a large extent still reflect different political conceptions of law, does not necessarily undermine their conventionality. As we noted earlier, the conventionality of the rules of recognition is easily reconcilable with their moral-political importance. Conventional practices of various kinds often evolve in response to historical contingencies, and their constitutive norms tend to reflect the normative convictions that were involved in the historical events that have brought to their existence. Conventions, as we have seen all along, are always supported by reasons. What makes norms conventional consists in the fact that those reasons underdetermine the content of the norms. But the reasons are still there, and there is nothing in the nature of those reasons that precludes the possibility that they reflect moral-political convictions. (Remember that even conventions of fashion reflect some aesthetic reasons or preferences, but that does not undermine their conventionality; and conventions of artistic genres reflect artistic reasons, conventions of games reflect reasons that we have for playing games, etc.)

Let me sum up: the conventional foundation of law consists of two layers. There are deep conventions that determine ways of organizing a legal order, its main building blocks, as it were, and those deep conventions are instantiated by the surface conventions of recognition that are specific to particular legal systems. The concept of law is constituted by both layers of conventions. Our concept of law partly depends on the deep conventions that determine the basic organization of a legal order, and partly on the specific institutions we have in our community, those that are determined by the rules of recognition. Both are conventional, and in this general insight, I think that Hart was quite right.

Bibliography

This bibliography lists all the works cited in the text. Dates cited are those of the edition used, not of first publication.

Anscombe, E. "Rules, Rights and Promises." *Midwest Studies in Philosophy* 3 (1978): 318.

Austin, J. L. *How to Do Things with Words.* Cambridge: Harvard University Press, 1962.

Bach, K., and R. Harnish. *Communication and Speech Acts.* Cambridge: MIT Press, 1979.

———. "How Performatives Really Work." *Linguistics and Philosophy* 15 (1992): 93.

Bacharach, M. *Beyond Individual Choice: Teams and Frames in Game Theory.* Ed. N. Gold and R. Sugden. Princeton: Princeton University Press, 2006.

Baker, G., and P. Hacker. *Wittgenstein, Meaning, and Understanding.* Oxford: Blackwell, 1980.

Bicchieri, C. *The Grammar of Society: The Nature and Dynamics of Social Norms.* Cambridge: Cambridge University Press, 2006.

Bratman, M. "Shared Agency." In *Faces of Intention*, 93. Cambridge: Cambridge University Press, 1999.

Brunero, J. "Two Approaches to Instrumental Rationality and Belief Consistency." *Journal of Ethics and Social Philosophy* 1, no 1 (2005), www.jesp.org.

Burge, T. "On Knowledge and Convention." *Philosophical Review* 84 (1975): 249.

Coleman, J. *The Practice of Principle.* Oxford: Oxford University Press, 2001.

Darwall, S. "Two Kinds of Respect." *Ethics* 88 (1997): 36.
Davis, W. *Meaning, Expression, and Thought.* Cambridge: Cambridge University Press, 2003.
den Hartogh, G. *Mutual Expectations: A Conventionalist Theory of Law.* New York: Kluwer, 2002.
Dickson, J. "Is the Rule of Recognition Really a Conventional Rule?" *Oxford Journal of Legal Studies* 27 (2007): 373.
Dworkin, R. M. *Justice in Robes.* Cambridge: Harvard University Press, 2006.
———. *Law's Empire.* London: Fontana, 1986.
———. *Taking Rights Seriously.* London: Duckworth, 1977.
Finnis, J. *Natural Law and Natural Rights.* Oxford: Oxford University Press, 1980.
Foucault, M. *The Order of Things: An Archeology of the Human Sciences.* New York: Random House, 1970.
Frankfurt, H. *The Importance of What We Care About.* Cambridge: Cambridge University Press, 1988.
Gallie, W. B. "Essentially Contested Concepts." *Proceedings of the Aristotelian Society* 56 (1956): 167.
Gans, C. "The Normativity of Law and Its Co-ordinative Function." *Israel Law Review* 16 (1981): 333.
Gilbert, M. *On Social Facts.* Princeton: Princeton University Press, 1989.
———. "Rationality, Coordination and Convention." *Synthese* 84 (1990): 1.
———. "Scanlon on Promissory Obligation: The Problem of Promisees' Rights." *Journal of Philosophy* 101 (2004): 83.
Goodman, N. *Fact, Fiction, and Forecast.* 3rd ed. Indianapolis: Bobbs-Merrill, 1973.
Green, L. "The Concept of Law Revisited." *Michigan Law Review* 94 (1996): 1687.
———. "Positivism and Conventionalism." *Canadian Journal of Law and Jurisprudence* 12 (1999): 35.
Grice, P. *Studies in the Way of Words.* Cambridge: Harvard University Press, 1989.
———. "Presupposition and Conversational Implicature." In *Radical Pragmatics*, ed. P. Cole, 183–97. New York: Academic Press, 1981.
Harman, G. "Moral Relativism." In *Moral Relativism and Moral Objectivity*, by G. Harman and J. J. Thomson. Cambridge, Mass.: Blackwell, 1996.

Hart, H.L.A. *The Concept of Law*. Oxford: Oxford University Press, 1961.

———. *The Concept of Law*. 2nd ed. Oxford: Oxford University Press, 1994.

Heuer, U. "Explaining Reasons: Where Does the Buck Stop?" *Journal of Ethics and Social Philosophy* 1, no. 3 (2006), www.jesp.org.

Hirsch, E, *Dividing Reality*. Oxford: Oxford University Press, 1993.

Hume, D. *A Treatise of Human Nature*. Ed. L. A. Selby-Brigge. 3rd ed., revised by P. H. Nidditch. Oxford: Oxford University Press, 1976.

Hurka, T. *Perfectionism*. Oxford: Oxford University Press, 1995.

Kaplan, D. "Demonstratives: An Essay on the Semantics, Logic, Metaphysics, and Epistemology of Demonstratives and Other Indexicals." In *Themes from Kaplan*, ed. J. Almog, J. Perry, and H. Wettstein, 481. Oxford: Oxford University Press, 1989.

Karttunen, L., and S. Peters. "Conventional Implicature." In *Syntax and Semantics*, vol. 11, *Presupposition*, ed. C. K. Oh and D. A. Dineen, 1. New York: Academic Press.

Kelsen, H. *General Theory of Law and State*. Trans. A. Wedberg. New York: Russell and Russell, 1961.

———. *Introduction to the Problems of Legal Theory: A Translation of the First Edition of the "Reine Rechtslehre" or "Pure Theory of Law."* Trans. B. L. Paulson and S. L. Paulson. Oxford: Oxford University Press, 1992.

———. *Pure Theory of Law*. 2nd ed. Trans. M. Knight. Berkeley and Los Angeles: University of California Press, 1967.

Kolodny, N., and J. Wallace. "Promises and Practices Revisited." *Philosophy and Public Affairs* 31 (2003): 119.

Kripke, S. *Wittgenstein on Rules and Private Language*. Oxford: Blackwell, 1982.

Lagerspetz, E. *The Opposite Mirrors: An Essay on the Conventionalist Theory of Institutions*. Boston: Kluwer, 1995.

Laurence, S. "A Chomskian Alternative to Convention-Based Semantics." *Mind* 105 (1996): 269.

Lemmon, E. J. "On Sentences Verifiable by Their Use." *Analysis* 22 (1962): 86.

Lewis, D. *Convention: A Philosophical Study*. Oxford: Blackwell, 1969.

———. "Languages and Language." In *Philosophical Papers*, vol 1. Oxford: Oxford University Press, 1983.

———. "Putnam's Paradox." *Australian Journal of Philosophy* 62 (1984): 221.

Ludlow, P., ed. *Readings in the Philosophy of Language*. Cambridge: MIT Press, 1997.

Marmor, A. "Deep Conventions." *Philosophy and Phenomenological Research* 74 (2007): 586.

———. "Do We Have a Right to Common Goods?" *Canadian Journal of Law and Jurisprudence* 14 (2001): 213.

———. "How Law Is Like Chess." *Legal Theory* 12 (2006): 347.

———. "Legal Positivism: Still Descriptive and Morally Neutral." *Oxford Journal of Legal Studies* 26 (2006): 683.

———. "On Convention." *Synthese* 107 (1996): 349.

———. *Positive Law and Objective Values*. Oxford: Oxford University Press, 2001.

McIntyre, A. *After Virtue: A Study in Moral Theory*. 2nd ed. London: Duckworth, 1985.

Miller, S. R. "Conventions, Interdependence of Action, and Collective Ends." *Nous* 20 (1986): 117.

———. "Rationalizing Conventions." *Synthese* 84 (1990): 23.

Millikan R. G. *Language: A Biological Model*. Oxford: Oxford University Press, 2005.

———. "Language Conventions Made Simple." *Journal of Philosophy* 95 (1998): 161.

Neale, S. "Context and Communication." In *Readings in the Philosophy of Language*, ed. Ludlow, 415. Cambridge: MIT Press, 1997.

Postema, G. "Coordination and Convention at the Foundations of Law." *Journal of Legal Studies* 11 (1982): 165.

Potts, C. *The Logic of Conventional Implicatures*. Oxford: Oxford University Press, 2005.

Putnam, H. "The Meaning of 'Meaning.'" In *Mind, Language, and Reality*. Cambridge: Cambridge University Press, 1975.

Quine, W. V. "Natural Kinds." In *Essays in Honor of Carl G. Hempel*, ed. N. Rescher, 1. Dordrecht: D. Reidel, 1970.

Rawls, J. *A Theory of Justice*. Cambridge: Harvard University Press, 1971.

Raz, J. *The Authority of Law*. Oxford: Oxford University Press, 1979.

———. "Moral Change and Social Relativism." *Social Philosophy and Policy* 11 (1994): 139.

———. *Practical Reason and Norms*. Princeton: Princeton University Press, 1990.

———. "Promises and Obligations." In *Law, Morality and Society: Essays in Honour of H. L. A. Hart*, ed. P. M. S. Hacker and J. Raz, 210. Oxford: Clarendon, 1977.

Rosch, E. H. "Natural Categories." *Cognitive Psychology* 4 (1973): 328.
Scanlon, T. "Promises and Practices." *Philosophy and Public Affairs* 19 (1990): 199.
———. *What We Owe to Each Other*. Cambridge: Harvard University Press, 1998.
Schwyzer, H. "Rules and Practices." *Philosophical Review* 78 (1969): 451.
Searle, J. *The Construction of Social Reality*. New York: Free Press, 1995.
———. *Expression and Meaning*. Cambridge: Cambridge University Press, 1979.
———. "How Performatives Work." *Linguistics and Philosophy* 12 (1989): 535.
———. "Literal Meaning." *Erkenntnis* 13 (1978): 207.
———. *Speech Acts*. Cambridge: Cambridge University Press, 1969.
Shafer-Landau, R. "Vagueness, Borderline Cases and Moral Realism." *American Philosophical Quarterly* 32 (1995): 83.
Soames, S. *Beyond Rigidity: The Unfinished Agenda of Naming and Necessity*. Oxford: Oxford University Press, 2002.
———. "Direct Reference, Propositional Attitudes, and Semantic Content." *Philosophical Topics* 15 (1987): 47.
———. "Drawing the Line between Meaning and Implicature—and Relating Both to Assertion." In *Philosophical Essays*, vol. 1. Princeton: Princeton University Press, 2009.
———. "Higher-Order Vagueness for Partially Defined Predicates." in *Liars and Heaps: New Essays on Paradox*, ed. J C Beall, 128. Oxford: Oxford University Press, 2003.
———. "Presupposition." In *Handbook of Philosophical Logic*, vol. 4, *Topics in the Philosophy of Language*, ed. D. Gabbay and F. Guenthner, 553. Dordrecht: Reidel.
———. *Understanding Truth*. Oxford: Oxford University Press, 1999.
Stalnaker, R. "Presuppositions." *Journal of Philosophical Logic* 2 (1973): 447.
Stalker, D., ed. *Grue! The New Riddle of Induction*. Chicago: Open Court, 1994.
Stanley, J., and T. Williamson. "Knowing How." *Journal of Philosophy* 98 (2001): 411.
Strawson, P. "Intention and Convention in Speech Acts." In *Logico-Linguistic Papers*, 170. London: Methuen, 1971.
Sugden, R. *The Economics of Rights, Co-operation, and Welfare*. 2nd ed. New York: Palgrave Macmillan, 2004.
Tuomela, R. *The Philosophy of Sociality*. Oxford: Oxford University Press, 2007.

Vanderschraaf, P. "Knowledge, Equilibrium, and Convention."
    Erkenntnis 49 (1998): 337.
Verbeek, B. "Conventions and Moral Norms: The Legacy of Lewis."
    Topoi 27 (2008): 73.
Warnock, G. J. *The Object of Morality*. London: Methuen, 1971.
Wittgenstein, L. *Philosophical Investigations*. Trans. G. E. M.
    Anscombe. Oxford: Blackwell, 1958.

Index

activity, rule-governed, 34–36
agreements, 4, 29
Aquinas, Thomas, 149
arbitrariness, x–xi, 1–2, 8–13, 26,
  42–44, 78, 166–67
arbitrary norms, 152
art: and constitutive conventions,
  37–38, 48–50; and deep conventions, 61–62, 64, 67–68; extension-
  range of term, 93–94
Austin, J. L., 80n2, 118, 139
awareness of conventionality, 5–8

Bach, K., 120–21, 125n31, 128
basic norm, 155, 159–60, 159n12
beliefs, 17, 67
Borges, Jorge Luis, 62–63
Bratman, Michael, 53n24
buck passing, 5n3
Burge, Tyler, 6

change, and deep conventions, 77–78
change process, for constitutive
  conventions, 47–49
charity, 152
chess, 14–15, 22–24, 23n29, 59,
  68–69, 89–91, 134–35; codification
  of, 50–51, 50n22; and constitutive
  rules, 42–43, 42n15–42n16; rules

of game, 160–61, 171; as social
  practice, 36–37, 40, 98; and values,
  38–39
civility, 140–41
codification, 50–52, 77
collective intentionality, 33n5, 53–54
common law, 173–74
community, concept of, 4–5
compliance, and social practice,
  41–42
compliance-dependent reasons,
  11–12, 26, 28, 41–42, 55
conditional reasons, and constitutive
  conventions, 142
consequentialism, 150
constitutive conventions, 32, 36–44;
  interpretive aspect of, 47–49;
  and moral reasons, 134–44; rules
  of recognition as, 165–71; and
  systems of rules, 45
constructivism, 38n12
contingency, 78, xi
conventional implicatures, 106–18
conventionality, defining, 2–19
conventional performatives, 130
conventions. *See* constitutive conventions; coordination conventions; deep conventions; surface
  conventions

conversational maxims, 107
cooperation, in social practices,
    52–57
coordination conventions, 32, 45,
    47–48, 62; and moral reasons,
    133–34; notation as, 82–83; and
    rules of recognition, 157, 165–71
coordination problem, 20–25, 20n25,
    30, 133; and norms of notation,
    82–83

deep conventions, 56–57; durability
    of, 77–78; elusiveness of, 74–75;
    and evaluative concepts, 147–48;
    instantiated in surface conven-
    tions, 75–77; in language, 94–96;
    of law, 171–75; and surface con-
    ventions, 58, 63–64, 66–67, 172.
    See also surface conventions
determinatio, 149
determining circumstances, 149–52
dictionaries, and encyclopedic codi-
    fication, 51
division of labor, and constitutive
    conventions, 46–47
dwindling of conventions, 3–4, 3n2
Dworkin, Ronald, 156, 162–63,
    162n17

encyclopedic codification, 50–52, 77
entrenchment, 70n10
essentially contested concepts, 54–55
evaluative concepts, 145–48
explicit performatives, 121–22
extension-range of meaning, 92–94

family resemblance concepts, 61n2,
    93, 98–99
following constitutive conventions,
    37
following rules, 6–8, 13–14, 32–35,
    38–39, 67; moral reasons for,
    132–44. See also rules
form of life, 63n6

Foucault, Michel, 62–63
Frankfurt, Henri, 142n12
friendship, 150–51, 153

Gallie, W. B., 54
games: and constitutive rules, 35n7;
    and deep conventions, 59–61, 66;
    as family resemblance concept,
    99–100; and norms, 68. See also
    chess
game theory, 20n25, 21
generalized conventional implica-
    tures, 109–12
general performatives, 130
Gilbert, Margaret, 3–4, 17n22,
    25–30
Goodman, N., 63n5, 70n10
grammar textbooks, and encyclope-
    dic codification, 51
Green, Leslie, 155, 166–67
Grice, P., 80n2, 106–13, 106n1
group fiat, 26–30
group identity, 26–27
grue, 63n5

Harman, Gilbert, 131n1
Harnish, R., 120–21, 125n31, 128
Hart, H.L.A., 51, 52n23, 155–56,
    160–62, 164
history, of constitutive conventions,
    49–50

identity, and constitutive rules, 43–44
imperfect duties, 150n15
implicatures, conventional, 106–18
implied content of utterance, 85–86
indeterminacy, 149–51
indifference, 8, 26
individuation, of norms/rules, 45n19
institutionalization, 51–52
institutional performatives, 122, 125,
    129–30
institutional practices, and codifica-
    tion, 51–52

internal goods, of social practices, 38n11
interpretation and change, in constitutive conventions, 47–49
invisible hand, 29–30
involuntary practices, 55–56

joint acceptance, 26–30
judges, disagreements on criteria of legality, 162–63

Kant, Immanuel, 150n15
Kelsen, Hans, 155, 158–60
knowing how, and following norm, 68–69
knowledge, partial, of constitutive conventions, 46–47
Kolodny, N., 140n10
Kripke, S., 87n11

Laurence, S., 82n7
law, deep conventions of, 171–75
legal conventionalism, 166
legal norms, 157–62
legal systems: and constitutive conventions, 46–47; families of, 172–74
legal validity, 155, 157–62
legislative codification, 50–52, 77
Lemmon, E. J., 120
Lewis, David, 4, 6, 8, 15–16, 19–25, 80n2, 156, 165
literal meaning, 63n6, 71n11, 84; practice-dependence of, 88–89; and semantic content, 84–86

maxims, conversational, 107
McIntyre, A., 38n11
meaning: and proper names, 105n28; of words, 83–96
measurement systems, 96–97
merkmal-definition, 102n14
Millikan, R. G., 25n30, 82n7
moral conventions, 144, 149–54

morality: and contingency, 131n1; and conventions, 131–54
moral reasons, to follow conventions, 132–44

naming, 83, 104. See also proper names
natural kind words, 102–3
Neal, Stephen, 115n17
Nix v. Hedden, 72, 103
norms, 67–77; alternative, 89; elements of, 45n19; use of term, 3n1
notation, 80–83

opting out, 55–56, 55n28, 142–44
ought statements, 158–61

path dependency, xi, 49–50, 78
performatives, 139–40. See also conventional performatives; explicit performatives; institutional performatives; statement-theory of performatives
performative utterances, 118–30
PGA v. Martin, 44n17
Piraha tribe, 88n12
Potts, Christopher, 116–17
practice, of conventions, 1–2
practice dependence, 10–11
practice theory: of promises, 136–40; of rules, 156, 161
pragmatics, and linguistic communication, 106–30
primary rules, 52n23
promises, practice theory of, 136–40
promising, 123–24, 124n31, 136–40
pronunciation, 82
proper names, 103–5, 105n28

quasi-agreement, 29–30
Quine, W., 19–20, 80n2

reasons, 75–77; compliance-dependent, 11–12, 26, 28, 41–42; to

reasons (*continued*)
follow conventions, 5–8, 10–12;
moral, 132–44
reciprocity, 28, 30
representation, as deep convention
of visual arts, 61–62
respect, 151. *See also* civility
rules, 13–17; arbitrariness of, 42–44;
constitutive, 31–36; informal,
15–16; regulative, 31–36; secondary, 51, 52n23; system of, 39, 45;
and values, 38–39
rules of recognition, 155–57, 160–62;
as conventions, 162–71; as surface
conventions, 172–74
rules of the road, 32–34

sanctions, for noncompliance, 52
Scanlon, T., 5n3, 137
Searle, John, 32–35, 33n5, 53–54,
63n6, 119, 123–26, 139
secondary rules, 51, 52n23
semantic content, 84–86
semantic implications, 112–15
shared agency, 53n24
similarity relations, 100–102, 101n22
single-criterion words, 96–98, 129
Soames, Scott, 106n1
social norms, 18–19
social practices, 36, 56; conventional,
34–36, 44–52; and cooperation,
53; nonidentity relation with
constitutive conventions, 40; and
systems of rules, 45
social rules, 3, 3n1
sound-sense relations in language,
80–83
sources of law, 155

speech acts, 139–40; conventions in,
118–30. *See also* performatives
spelling conventions, 47, 48n21
standing in line, 33
Stanley, J., 68
statement-theory of performatives,
120–21, 126–29, 139–40
Strawson, P., 120
surface conventions: degrees of
shallowness, 65; distinguished
from deep conventions, 172; and
evaluative concepts, 147–48; and
instantiation of deep conventions,
63–64, 75–77
syntax, 79, 79n1
system of rules, 39, 45

tacit understandings, 16
theater, 37–39, 49–50, 65–66
translation, difficulties of, 70–72, 74

underdeterminacy by reasons, 78, xi
U.S. Constitution, 170

vagueness: degrees of, 95n16; and
family resemblance, 102; in language, 91–92
values, and constitutive conventions,
36–44
Verbeek, Bruno, 10n10
visual arts, 61, 64–65
voluntary practices, 55–56

Wallace, J., 140n10
Williamson, Tim, 42n16, 68
Wittgenstein, Ludwig, 61n2, 63n6,
80n2, 87n11, 98–99
words, meaning of, 83–96

CPSIA information can be obtained
at www.ICGtesting.com
Printed in the USA
BVOW08s1141090917
494423BV00001B/35/P